Business Continuity in a Cyber World

Business Continuity in a Cyber World

Surviving Cyberattacks

David Sutton

BUSINESS EXPERT PRESS

Business Continuity in a Cyber World: Surviving Cyberattacks
Copyright © Business Expert Press, LLC, 2018.

First published in 2018 by
Business Expert Press, LLC
222 East 46th Street, New York, NY 10017
www.businessexpertpress.com

ISBN-13: 978-1-94744-146-0 (paperback)
ISBN-13: 978-1-94744-147-7 (e-book)

Business Expert Press Information Systems Collection

Collection ISSN: 2156-6577 (print)
Collection ISSN: 2156-6593 (electronic)

Cover and interior design by S4Carlisle Publishing Services Private Ltd., Chennai, India

First edition: 2018

10 9 8 7 6 5 4 3 2 1

Printed in the United States of America.

Abstract

Until recently, if it has been considered at all in the context of business continuity, cybersecurity may have been thought of in terms of disaster recovery and little else. Recent events have shown that cyberattacks are now an everyday occurrence, and it is becoming clear that the impact of these can have devastating effects on organizations whether large and small, and whether in the public or the private sector.

Cybersecurity is one aspect of information security, since the impacts or consequences of a cyberattack will inevitably damage one or more of the three pillars of information security: the confidentiality, integrity, or availability of an organization's information assets. The main difference between information security and cybersecurity is that while information security deals with all types of information assets, cybersecurity deals purely with those that are accessible by means of interconnected electronic networks, including the Internet.

Many responsible organizations now have robust information security, business continuity, and disaster recovery programs in place, and it is not the intention of this book to rewrite those, but to inform organizations about the kind of precautions they should take to stave off successful cyberattacks and how they should deal with them when they arise in order to protect their day-to-day business.

Keywords

availability, compromise, confidentiality, continuity, cyber, cyber threat, cyberattack, cybersecurity, denial of service, information security, integrity, prevention, response, risk

Contents

Acknowledgments...ix

Introduction...xi

Chapter 1   The Practice of Business Continuity Management.............1

Chapter 2   A Brief Overview of the Risk Management Process 11

Chapter 3   The Main Cybersecurity Issues 25

Chapter 4   Information Assets and Impacts 35

Chapter 5   Vulnerabilities and Threats 47

Chapter 6   Selecting Strategic, Tactical, and
             Operational Solutions 61

Chapter 7   Business Continuity Activities and Solutions....................79

Chapter 8   Testing, Exercising, and Maintaining Plans 109

Chapter 9   Embedding Cybersecurity and Business Continuity 123

Appendix A Information on Cybersecurity Controls.........................131

Appendix B Standards and Good Practice Guidelines........................149

Glossary 163

Bibliography...169

About the Author..171

Index 173

Acknowledgments

I would like to take this opportunity to thank:

My wife Sharon for her unceasing support throughout all my writing work;

My children Bella, Matt, and James and their respective partners for their continuing encouragement, and my wonderful grandchildren for regularly helping me remember that there's much more to life than work;

My good friend and colleague Andy Taylor, who put me in touch with BEP in the first place, Nigel Wyatt, for forwarding my abstract, and Scott Isenberg, for agreeing to publish the book;

Finally, Mr. Evans, my English teacher at Thomas Adams School in Wem, for reasons that I hope will be obvious.

Introduction

Why Is Business Continuity Important?

From 2003 to 2014, I gave an annual lecture on business continuity to information security students studying for their master's degree at the Royal Holloway University of London. On one occasion and before I had even begun the lecture, a particularly difficult student (there's always one, isn't there?) asked me what business continuity had to do with information security. I explained that if he listened for a few minutes all would become clear. This he did, albeit rather grumpily.

After my introductory slides, I explained with several real-world examples just what can happen to an organization when information assets are damaged, stolen, or rendered unavailable. The point I was trying to get over was that it wasn't only about the information and the systems that held it, but everything around that as well—the computer room and its supporting infrastructure; the building and its immediate environment; neighboring buildings; the weather; the political and economic constraints; and by no means least the people, and how a bizarre chain of events can sometimes contrive to cause unexpected problems.

One of my best examples related to an explosion at an oil storage depot a little way northwest of London in December 2005.[1] The explosion in itself was a major event, requiring the fire and rescue services of three counties to control and extinguish the subsequent fires, but it was a building several hundred metres away that suffered the particular information security impact. The heat from the fire was so intense that it caused a large and heavy air-conditioning unit fixed to the ceiling of the computer room to break loose and fall directly onto an even larger and more expensive mainframe which was processing extremely sensitive data. Unsurprisingly, the mainframe failed, but fortunately the disaster recovery system located about 30 miles away cut in immediately and both the data and the reputation of the organization were saved.

---

[1]See http://www.hse.gov.uk/research/rrpdf/rr718.pdf

When thinking about protecting an organization's information assets, it's always worthwhile asking one simple question: "What could possibly go wrong?"

Could, for example, a loosely affiliated group of hackers take down the CIA's website? Yes. A group known as Anonymous did so in 2012[2]— it was not the first time this had happened. Clearly, the CIA was able to respond quickly, and although it did not suffer any financial loss as a result, it did lose face.

Could another hacking group develop a piece of malware that encrypted the hard disk drives of systems all over the world and demand a ransom to unencrypt them? Yes—the WannaCry virus (attributed to North Korea) in 2017 did just this. Many organizations were totally unprepared for this kind of attack and suffered financial, operational, and reputational losses as a result.

Could a major government department still be using personal computers running Windows XP, 7 years after it had ceased to be supported by Microsoft? Again, yes—but on this occasion, I will spare them the embarrassment of naming them!

The answer then to the question "What could possibly go wrong?" is "Almost anything one could imagine, and quite a few things one might never have even thought of."

Twenty years ago, no one could reasonably have imagined the aforementioned examples, but today all bets are off, and nothing would surprise me anymore.

So, what is the problem? Is it a lack of understanding of the issues at senior management level? Is it a lack of investment in securing an organization's systems and services against cyber threats? Is it a lack of training of IT and security personnel? Is it a lack of awareness of users? Is it the result of work by extremely clever attackers? Is it the poor security design of IT systems and services? Actually, it is a combination of all of these, and possibly many more.

In recent years, an unprecedented number of major business-disrupting cyber incidents have occurred. Some of the organizations affected by

---

[2]See http://www.telegraph.co.uk/news/worldnews/northamerica/usa/9076314/CIA-website-hacked-in-attack-claimed-by-shadowy-cyber-group-Anonymous.html

these have survived them; others have not. The key to ensuring that your organization remains in the former category rather than the latter is a combination of information security or cybersecurity, and business continuity management, an increasingly important aspect of business life, but one that is frequently overlooked.

Why Should You Read This Book?

This book will not teach you how to become either a seasoned business continuity practitioner or a cybersecurity specialist; only time, training, and experience can accomplish these, but hopefully the book will point you in the right direction. It should not be thought of as a substitute for formal training for which there are many excellent courses available, but more as a guide to enable you to ask the right questions and as a result to make the right decisions.

Although it is now 5 years old, the International Standards Organisation's (ISO's) ISO 22301 is still the widely accepted business continuity standard, and some people will say that you should get to know it as soon as possible; well maybe not quite at this stage. ISO 22301 is rather like a manufacturer's maintenance manual in the context of learning to drive a car. You don't need a detailed knowledge of it in order to learn how to drive—and maybe not even afterward. You do, however, need to understand the mechanics of how to make the car go (and stop), change direction, and a hundred and one other things.

Likewise, you do not need to understand how to tailor the rules of a network firewall or modify the detailed security settings within a major business application, but you will find it useful to understand what the key issues are, and at least at a high level, how to deal with them.

If, in the fullness of time, you become a key player in your organization's cybersecurity program, or even become the organization's business continuity manager, then you will definitely need to understand the standards—and there are quite a few that might be relevant—but for the time being we shall discuss them briefly in a later chapter and provide additional detail in the appendices.

While it does not follow either publication to the letter, this book is based somewhat loosely around the Business Continuity Institute's Good

Practice Guidelines 2018, which have been updated to include cybersecurity issues, and the ISO's ISO 22301:2012, which deals with the requirements for business continuity management systems. This was produced at a time when cybersecurity awareness was less well publicized than it is today, and hence does not deal with the issues directly, so I have also included relevant details from ISO/International Electrotechnical Commission (IEC) 27001:2017, which addresses the requirements for information security management systems together with its partner standard ISO/IEC 27002:2017, which defines the code of practice for information security controls.

This book—as its title suggests—aims to bring into a single source the closely interrelated disciplines of cybersecurity and business continuity, deals with the effects that cyber threats can have on an organization, and recommends steps that organizations can take to mitigate the risks.

The book won't provide the reader with the fine detail needed to prevent or minimize the problems; that can be found in other more technical books,[3] but it will highlight the general steps that organizations can take, so that they are better prepared for when disruptive incidents arise and are able to deal with them swiftly, efficiently, and without there being an adverse effect on the organization's brand, business, or public image.

What Do We Mean by Terms Related to Cyber?

While many people would imagine that it is a relatively recent term, *cyber* has actually been around colloquially since 1982, when the American science fiction author William Gibson coined the term *cyberspace* in a short story entitled "Burning Chrome",[4] but he did not define it until 2 years later in his book *Neuromancer*[5] in which he describes it:

> Cyberspace. A consensual hallucination experienced daily by billions of legitimate operators, in every nation...a graphic

---

[3]See D. Sutton. 2017. *Cyber Security: A practitioner's guide* (Swindon, UK: BCS). ISBN 978-1-78017-340-5

[4]W. Gibson. 1982. *Burning Chrome* (New York, NY: Omni magazine).

[5]W. Gibson. 1984. *Neuromancer* (New York, NY: Ace books).

representation of data from the banks of every computer in the human system. Unthinkable complexity. Lines of light ranged in the nonspace of the mind, clusters and constellations of data.

Bearing in mind that this predates the development of the World Wide Web by Sir Tim Berners-Lee at CERN (the European Organization for Nuclear Research) in 1990 by 6 years, it is an extremely insightful concept.

The Global Cyber Definitions Database[6] defines the term *cyber* as "almost invariably the prefix for a term or the modifier of a compound word, rather than a stand-alone word. Its inference usually relates to electronic information (data) processing, information technology, electronic communications (data transfer) or information and computer systems."[7]

Cyberspace is succinctly defined by the Department of Homeland Security as "the interdependent network of information technology infrastructures, that includes the Internet, telecommunications networks, computer systems, and embedded processors and controllers."[8]

Cybercrime is defined as "criminal activity conducted using computers and the Internet, often financially motivated. Cybercrime includes identity theft, fraud, and internet scams, among other activities. Cybercrime is distinguished from other forms of malicious cyber activity, which have political, military, or espionage motivations."[9]

A *cyberattack* is "an attack, via cyberspace, targeting an enterprise's use of cyberspace for the purpose of disrupting, disabling, destroying, or maliciously controlling a computing environment/infrastructure; or destroying the integrity of the data or stealing controlled information."[10]

Cyber warfare is defined as "cyber-attacks that are authorized by state actors against cyber infrastructure in conjunction with a government campaign."[11]

---

[6]See http://cyberdefinitions.newamerica.org

[7]See https://www.turvallisuuskomitea.fi/index.php/en/yhteiskunnan-turvallisuusstrategia-yts

[8]See http://niccs.us-cert.gov/glossary

[9]See http://www.dpc.senate.gov/docs/fs-112-2-183.pdf

[10]See http://nvlpubs.nist.gov/nistpubs/ir/2013/NIST.IR.7298r2.pdf

[11]See http://www.ewi.info/idea/critical-terminology-foundations-2

Cyber harassment has been defined as "the use of Information and Communications Technology (ICT) to harass, control, manipulate or habitually disparage a child, adult, business or group without a direct or implied threat of physical harm."[12] It includes cyber bullying, cyber stalking, false accusation, victimization and posting such things as racist, homophobic, defamatory, or derogatory comments.

The *Encyclopedic Dictionary of Public Administration* defines *cyber surveillance* as "a mechanism for the surveillance of persons, objects or processes that is based on new technologies and that is operated from and on data networks such as the Internet."[13]

Finally, *cybersecurity* is "the ability to protect or defend the use of cyberspace from cyber-attacks."[14] This refers to information security as it is applied to cyberspace and is, therefore, slightly different from the wider concept of information security, which also includes tangible as well as intangible information.

Organization of the Book

The book is divided into nine main chapters. Furthermore, there are two appendices, a bibliography, and a glossary that provide additional supporting information.

Chapter 1 provides an introduction to the practice of business continuity management and its key focus in relation to cybersecurity. It describes the need for and the benefits of business continuity within organizations.

Chapter 2 provides a review of the underlying generic risk management process. A risk management approach underpins both the entire business continuity and the cybersecurity management processes. This chapter provides a review (as opposed to a detailed description) of risk management practice and explains the terminology used.

In **Chapter 3**, we examine the main cyber-related issues that cause business disruption—cybercrime, cyber harassment, cyber warfare, cyber surveillance, and cybersecurity failures.

---

[12]See https://www.ipredator.co/cyber-harassment

[13]See www.dictionnaire.enap.ca/dictionnaire/docs/definitions/definitions_anglais/cyber_surveillance.pdf

[14]See http://nvlpubs.nist.gov/nistpubs/ir/2013/NIST.IR.7298r2.pdf

Chapter 4 discusses how we might identify the organization's information assets and their value. These information assets, together with the systems and networks that underpin them, are key to the ongoing ability of all organizations to operate successfully, and therefore a detailed understanding of them is required. This chapter describes the kind of assets most organizations possess and how to make a meaningful estimate of their value through the impact that their loss, damage, or destruction might cause.

Chapter 5 deals with the potential vulnerabilities that might enable a successful cyberattack against the organization's assets and the threats that can take advantage of them.

In **Chapter 6**, we move to determine and implement an overall cyberattack prevention and response strategy. Once organizations have a clear understanding of their information assets and their value, they will be better placed to begin development of a strategy that will form the basis of action plans.

This chapter will deal with the two principal areas:

Prevention—the proactive side of business continuity and cybersecurity, which aims either to reduce the likelihood of a successful cyberattack by putting measures in place that stop such an attack or to reduce the impact of a successful attack.

Response—the reactive side of business continuity and cybersecurity, which aims to equip the organization for reacting quickly to a cyberattack that is not stopped by preventative measures but limits its impact and enables the organization to return as quickly as possible to a normal or near-normal operational status. Equally importantly, the response strategy also deals with how the organization should communicate with its customers, stakeholders, and, where necessary, government or sector authorities and regulators.

Chapter 7 examines the actual business continuity activities and solutions to cybersecurity problems. It covers the steps that organizations can take proactively to minimize or prevent successful cyberattacks, major activities such as disaster recovery, and finally how organizations should go about responding to disruptive incidents.

The chapter continues by describing how organizations should implement the preventative measures and turn the response strategies into contingency plans to be used when required.

In **Chapter 8**, we look at the methods of exercising, testing, maintaining, and reviewing plans relating to the cybersecurity aspects of the business continuity function.

An untested plan is not really a plan at all, and this chapter deals with various types of test and exercise that an organization might undertake in order to validate the effectiveness of its cybersecurity plans. It also covers the process of reviewing the results of tests and exercises in order to improve the plans in readiness for responding to real cybersecurity incidents.

Finally, in **Chapter 9**, we discuss embedding the culture of the cybersecurity and business continuity across the whole organization.

Unfortunately, some of any organizations' greatest risks arise from individual users of information services within the organization itself. This chapter represents the final piece in the business continuity jigsaw—that of embedding the business continuity culture across the whole organization, so that it becomes a part of everybody's daily responsibility and enables the organization's users to be both a first line and a last line of defense against cyberattacks.

The **appendices** include the following:

- Information on controls suitable for treating cybersecurity issues;
- Links to national and international Standards and Good Practice Guidelines.
- These are followed by the bibliography and glossary, which is a brief description of commonly used business continuity and cybersecurity terminology.

Author's note:

After I sent the manuscript of this book to the publisher in early 2018, the Cambridge Analytica story went from "interesting" to "sensational" in a very short space of time. I had not included any reference to it in the book, simply because at the time it did not appear to constitute a significant cybersecurity issue. In hindsight of course, it most definitely does.

As the debate will doubtless continue well beyond the book's publication, it would be pointless to speculate about the possible social, technical, and political repercussions, but what appear to be indisputable are the links between Cambridge Analytica, its parent group SCL, Aggregate IQ, Facebook, politicians on both sides of the Atlantic, and the misuse of millions of individuals' personal information.

While you may think that your personal information is safe, think again—it most certainly is not, and you should not be surprised if so-called reputable organizations use it in ways you neither expected nor agreed to. The individual people and corporations who are responsible for this may say "sorry", but whether they mean it or whether they will face any form of punishment remains to be seen.

Paraphrasing the words of the philosopher George Santayana, "Those who refuse to take account of the past are destined to repeat it."

CHAPTER 1

The Practice of Business Continuity Management

This chapter will introduce the concept of business continuity management with a particular reference to cybersecurity. It will describe the need for, and the benefits of, business continuity within all kinds of organizations and will cover some basic business continuity terminology.

What Exactly Is Business Continuity Management?

Many people think that business continuity is all about protecting the future of the organization against some form of disruption. This is perfectly true, but it's also about protecting the organization's past history and its current position, and it's worthwhile spending a few moments developing these points.

Firstly, most if not all organizations depend upon their reputation in order to survive and grow. Once an organization's reputation becomes tarnished, it is very difficult—some might say even impossible—to repair the damage and regain the organization's reputation and standing to what it was before things went wrong. For example, how easy would it be to trust an organization that has released sensitive personal details of your life, regardless of whether the release was accidental or deliberate?

Secondly, most disruptive incidents—especially cyber incidents—will have an immediate effect. A denial of service attack, as we shall see later, can stop an organization's online trading in seconds and with it that organization's ability to continue to deliver its online products or services ceases.

Thirdly, even if an organization can recover from whatever has caused the disruption, the first two factors—loss of reputation and damage to its current trading position—might well mean that future trading or delivery of services is impossible.

Business continuity takes the view that all three areas must be addressed, and does so in a clear and concise manner:

- To begin with, the business continuity practitioner must understand how the organization functions; what its key objectives are; how it attains these; and what will be the impact or consequence if it cannot do so. This is covered in greater detail in Chapter 4.
- The next step is to understand the vulnerabilities and threats to which the organization is exposed; the likelihood that the threats will be carried out; and therefore, the level of risk the organization faces. We address this aspect of business continuity in Chapter 5.
- Following this, the organization must decide on the most appropriate methods of treating the risks, which may be one or more of

  - avoiding the risk;
  - sharing it with another organization;
  - reducing the risk;
  - accepting some level of residual risk.

This is covered in Chapter 6; in Chapter 7 how the organization must implement the risk treatment method chosen; and finally in Chapter 8 verify that the treatment has been successful.

Why Should Organizations Practice Business Continuity?

To most people, the answer to this question should appear obvious, but it is a matter of continuing amazement that some organizations simply don't see the point.

Perhaps the most dangerous attitude is the view that "it hasn't happened to us in the past, so it probably won't happen in the future." The outcome of this view could only ever go one of two ways, and if organizations that think it's going to swing in their favor, they are likely to be in for a surprise, especially in the highly unpredictable world of cyber disruptions.

Another common view is that business continuity is expensive, that it reduces an organization's revenues and therefore its profits. Once an organization understands that the cost of prevention is normally far less than the cost of the disruption itself, together with the cost of correcting the disruption, this view is more easily overcome.

A much more positive argument is that business continuity can improve an organization's profitability, since its customers and trading partners are much more likely to wish to do business with the organization if it can show that it takes business continuity seriously. Indeed, in some sectors, demonstrating an organization's business continuity capability or accreditation to a national or international standard may be a legal or contractual requirement.

How This Relates to Cybersecurity

Although business continuity and cybersecurity are two somewhat different disciplines, we shall see throughout the remainder of this book that they are actually inextricably connected. The reason for this is twofold:

Firstly, we need to understand how cyber-related disruptions can impact an organization's normal day-to-day operations, and secondly, we must appreciate how other disruptive (non-cyber-related) incidents can impact an organization's cyber activities.

There is also a belief when discussing business continuity and cybersecurity that the solution must be disaster recovery, but as we shall see in Chapter 7, disaster recovery is just one method of dealing with risk as part of an overall risk management plan.

The Importance of Senior Management Buy-In

It is often the case that people lower down an organization see the need for some form of business continuity, but have difficulty convincing those higher up that it is a worthwhile idea. This issue is dealt with in Chapter 2, where we discuss business cases and how these can be used to inform senior management, obtain their buy-in to the concept of a business continuity program, and ensure not only that funds are available to cover the costs but also that all levels within the organization become aware of and part of the program.

A Few Words on Standards

Standards, specifications, guidelines, and recommendations are all written with the express purpose of ensuring that things are designed, produced, and delivered to a uniform level of quality, and so that something produced to meet a given standard in one country will be compatible with something produced elsewhere. At a fundamental level, that's it, so let's take a closer look at the definitions of these terms.

Standards

Standards and specifications are **directive** tell you what should be done; guidelines and recommendations are **informative**, and tell you how you should go about it. The Merriam-Webster dictionary defines Standard[1] as "something set up and established by authority as a rule for the measure of quantity, weight, extent, value, or quality"; and "something established by authority, custom, or general consent as a model or example."

Some standards bodies produce their output for local consumption only, whereas the larger ones tend to produce output intended for more widespread use. An example of the former category is the Singapore Standards Council, whose output is generally used solely within that country. An example of the second category is the British Standards Institute, which has been at the forefront of standards development since 1901, and much of its output is utilized worldwide, often being turned into truly international standards by the ISO.

In some countries, it is possible for an organization to be formally accredited against a standard, providing that organization with proof that its business practice meets or exceeds the level required by the standard.

Specifications

A specification is defined as "an act of identifying something precisely or of stating a precise requirement"; and "a detailed description of the design and materials used to make something."

---

[1] See https://www.merriam-webster.com/dictionary/standard

Guidelines

A guideline is defined as "a general rule, principle, or piece of advice."

Recommendations

A recommendation is defined as "a suggestion or proposal as to the best course of action, especially one put forward by an authoritative body."

Good Practice Guidelines

There are also so-called Good Practice documents, which rather than being issued by a standards body, originate from an organization that has a legitimate claim to be the main source of knowledge on matters pertaining to it.

Regardless of their name or definition, standards, specifications, guidelines, and recommendations are costly to produce and tend to be developed and distributed by large international organizations that usually make a charge, or by government departments, which may subsidize them to a greater or lesser degree.

At the time of writing, there are two principal documents with which we should become familiar. The first is the Business Continuity Institute's (BCI's) Good Practice Guidelines 2018, which although not an international standard, is widely accepted as an excellent source of knowledge and information on the subject. The second is from ISO 22301:2012—Societal security—Business continuity management systems—Requirements.

For the beginner in business continuity, the BCI Good Practice Guidelines (GPG) 2018 is very much the best place to start. Apart from providing considerable detail about how to go about the business continuity process, it has the great advantage of being relatively inexpensive to buy. ISO 22301 (to give it its abbreviated title), on the other hand, is considerably more costly and is much less detailed, dealing only with the essentials, and making the assumption that the reader is already familiar with the practice of business continuity. It is, therefore, aimed more at the more experienced practitioner.

Unfortunately, until you purchase a Standards document, it's difficult to assess how useful it is likely to be to you, and often the descriptions provided on the Standards' websites do not give the potential buyer much of a flavor of what is inside. In Appendix B of this book, we shall examine both the BCI's GPG 2018 and ISO 22301 in a little more detail, and we'll also take a brief look at a number of other business continuity and information security standards.

Plan-Do-Check-Act

Like many subjects involving the risk management process, the business continuity standards follow the frequently used Plan-Do-Check-Act principle, also known as the Deming cycle.

Plan

In the first stage, we establish the objectives and processes necessary to deliver results in accordance with the expected output (the target or goals). By establishing output expectations, the completeness and accuracy of the work is also a part of the proposed improvement.

Do

In the second stage, we implement the plan or carry out the activity, collecting data for analysis in the following Check and Act steps.

Check

In the third stage, we study the actual results (measured and collected in Do) and compare them against the expected results (targets or goals from the Plan) to identify any differences. We look for any deviations from the plan and also for its appropriateness and completeness.

Act

In the fourth and final stage, sometimes called the Adjust stage, we undertake corrective actions on significant differences between actual and planned results, by analyzing the differences to determine their root causes and determining where to apply changes that will include improvement of the process.

Business Continuity Terminology

As with any specialist subject, business continuity makes use of some terminology with which readers may not be immediately familiar.

Maximum Tolerable Period of Disruption (MTPD)

The maximum tolerable period of disruption, referred to as MTPD or MTPoD, is the time it would take for the impact arising from a disruptive incident to be deemed unacceptable.

This is a fairly fundamental measurement—it could be very short, in the case of organizations that provide a real-time service such as an Internet banking, where the customer needs 24-hour access to his or her money and banking facilities. Other services can be unavailable for much longer periods of time without great impact, but there will come a point in time beyond which the organization is unable to survive.

The MTPD will be a major factor in determining the continuity requirements that we shall discuss in Chapter 7.

Recovery Time Objective (RTO)

While the MTPD defines the absolute limit of disruption the organization can endure, it will often be desirable to recover some proportion of activities or services prior to this deadline. Many organizations would be happy to be able to recover say 50 percent of their capacity fairly rapidly following an incident, and gradually build back up to the 100 percent that existed prior to the incident.

This then is the recovery time objective (RTO), and is the period of time following a disruptive incident within which resumption of activities or recovery of resources must be well under way, even if incomplete.

The actual process of recovery will clearly have to begin well before the RTO point, and part of the organization's business continuity plan will have to account for an initial loss of productivity followed by a gradual increase to the level required at RTO.

The ISO standard states that, for products, services, and activities, the RTO must be less than the time it would take for the adverse impacts that would arise as a result of not providing a product/service or performing an activity to become unacceptable. In simple terms, this means that the RTO must always be less than the MTPD.

Recovery Point Objective (RPO)

The RPO is the target time for the worst-case data loss in planning terms, and is defined as the point to which information must be recovered to enable the activity to resume. Essentially, this usually refers to the point at which the last data backup activity was carried out.

Maximum Tolerable Data Loss (MTDL)

Although MTDL is widely used in business continuity circles, neither ISO 22301 nor the BCI's GPG 2018 actually defines it. However, it may be critical to organizations in the cyber context, in which case as useful a definition as any would be "the maximum loss of information (electronic and other data) which an organisation can tolerate, the value of which could make operational recovery impossible or be so substantial as to put the organisation's business viability at risk."

Minimum Business Continuity Objective (MBCO)

The Minimum Business Continuity Objective (MBCO) is defined as the minimum acceptable level for the organization to achieve its objectives during a disruptive incident.

The term has similar connotations to RTO, in that while RTO refers to time, MBCO refers to the level of capability. An example of this would be an organization normally operating three information processing systems and which knows that it can maintain a basic level of service by running just two systems if the third is out of action.

Continuity Requirements Analysis

The final piece of terminology is the continuity requirements analysis, in which we look back at the business impact analysis, and take from that the activities we most need to undertake in order to bring about recovery and restoration of services, and the timescales in which we would like to achieve them.

Information Security Terminology

Before we look further into risk management itself, let us quickly review some of the key terms that are particularly relevant to cybersecurity.

Confidentiality

Confidentiality involves ensuring that information is not made available or disclosed to individuals (including entities and processes) who are not authorized to view it. The implication of this is that we must ensure that we have adequate safeguards in place to restrict access to information to only those individuals who have a genuine need to have access to it. A good example of this is in a doctor's surgery, where the doctors and nurses would require full access to a patient's medical records, whereas the receptionist would not.

Integrity

Integrity follows on from confidentiality in situations where individuals do have the right to access information, and ensures that they are unable to modify it without further authorization. For example, it may be perfectly acceptable for university students to access their assignment or examination results, but they should not be permitted to change the grades!

Availability

Availability is the cybersecurity concept that is totally aligned to business continuity. It requires information to be accessible and usable by authorized individuals at agreed times, and it is when information becomes unavailable that businesses really begin to suffer. Consider the case of a major UK banking group during the summer of 2012. Changes made to their online systems did not work as expected, leaving customers unable to access their accounts, and unable to receive payments made into their accounts by other banks. This particularly affected organizations that were trying to pay their staff and house buyers attempting to complete the final purchase process.

Authentication

Authentication is a means of establishing beyond reasonable doubt that an individual is who he or she claims to be. Authentication comes in many forms—for example a shared secret such as a password, or sometimes additionally as a passcode from an electronic token. More recently, biometric methods have become a popular means of authentication, and manufacturers have introduced fingerprint authentication and facial recognition in consumer electronics.

Nonrepudiation

Nonrepudiation is the term that defines that an individual who has made authorized alterations to information should not be able to deny having done so, and neither should the system holding the information be able to indicate otherwise. Nonrepudiation provides an audit trail, which can demonstrate (again, beyond reasonable doubt) that an individual has for example, ordered goods online, or paid a bill.

Summary

In this chapter, we have discussed what business continuity is used for and why organizations should practice it, how this relates to cybersecurity, and how the organization's senior management must buy into the concept. We have also touched briefly on the need for standards, and explained some of the most important business continuity terminology.

In the next chapter, we will provide a brief overview of the risk management process.

CHAPTER 2

A Brief Overview of the Risk Management Process

A risk management approach underpins the entire business continuity and cybersecurity management processes. This chapter will provide a review (as opposed to a detailed description) of generic risk management practice. There are many publications on risk management—books, white papers, and Standards, and a number of these are listed in Bibliography.

Where Risk Management Is Used

People from different occupational backgrounds will view the term "risk management" in quite different ways. Some organizations view risk as an opportunity—usually to make money, for example, in the case of an investment bank considering funding a start-up operation. Others will see risk as having negative connotations, and it is this view that is relevant in both cybersecurity and business continuity.

ISO Guide73:2009 defines risk management as "coordinated activities to direct and control an organisation with regard to risk." Anyone who undertakes business continuity work in an information technology environment will also be familiar with the term "disaster recovery," and if we view this together with cybersecurity and business continuity, we might see that each of the three disciplines makes extensive use of risk management in order to understand what we are trying to protect and why.

What Is Risk?

Risk is at the very heart of business continuity, but when we talk about risk, it is easy to misunderstand the terminology, so let's begin by looking briefly at its various components.

Risk is actually a combination of the impact or consequence of something happening and the likelihood or probability that it will happen. The impact or consequence comes as the result of a threat acting upon an asset of some kind, where that asset has a degree of vulnerability, and where that vulnerability gives rise to the likelihood or probability.

Figure 2.1 illustrates this.

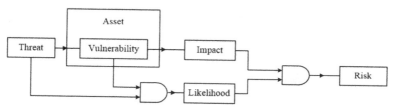

Figure 2.1 A general view of the risk environment

Let's look at a simple example.

If a computer is not protected with a password, anyone who has access to it can either steal the machine, and/or read, copy, change, or delete any of the application software or data on it. The machine itself, the application software, or data represent the assets; the threat is that some unauthorized and ill-intentioned person may obtain access to the machine and undertake some detrimental activity as a result; the vulnerability is the lack of password protection; the impact or consequence would be the damage to or loss of machine, software, or data. Separately, the likelihood will depend upon the attacker knowing or guessing that the machine is unprotected and having the desire to recover or remove software or data from it. The result is the risk.

Therefore: Risk = Impact or consequence × Likelihood or probability

All the same, even if the machine is protected with a password, there still exists the possibility that an attacker will try to guess or recover the password to gain access. The impact remains the same, although the like-lihood is somewhat reduced.

Understanding risk and planning for how to deal with it is known as risk management. There are five main components to this as shown in Figure 2.2 (taken from the international standard ISO/IEC 27005:2011—Information security risk management), and we'll look briefly at each in turn, and expand on them later in the chapter.

Context Establishment

This simply means gaining an understanding of the organization; how it operates; the environment in which it operates; its key objectives, products, or services; and which of these are liable to cause disruption to the organization if they cannot be achieved or delivered.

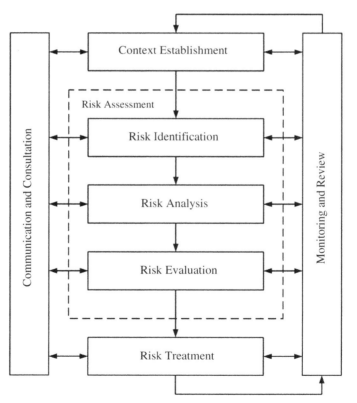

Figure 2.2 The overall process of risk management

Within this, it is also important to understand the organization's *risk appetite*. This is the level of risk the organization will accept for any individual asset or activity. For example, it may decide not to insure low-value items as the cost of doing so might outweigh the possible benefits. At the other end of the risk appetite scale, the organization may decide that the possible failure of a high-cost project could affect its survivability, and that it should not go ahead. Somewhere between these two arbitrary points will lie the organization' risk appetite for any given asset or activity.

Risk Assessment

This next stage of the risk management process comprises three separate steps.

Risk identification is (as shown in Figure 2.2) the process of identifying the various assets, the threats that they might face, the impacts or consequences of their being disrupted, the vulnerabilities that they possess, and finally the likelihood or probability that one or more of the threats might be carried out.

Threats may arise from a variety of sources—man-made or natural, and there are some that we as individuals or organizations can do little or nothing about, for example the threat of a hacking attack or a flood. We may be able to reduce the impact if threats take place, or possible to reduce the likelihood that they will occur, but the threats will always remain.

Chapter 5 deals in much greater detail with the kinds of cyber threats we are likely to encounter, but also briefly covers noncyber threats that can nonetheless result in an impact on an organization's cyber activities.

Impacts or *consequences* represent one part of the risk equation, and may also take many forms. They can be financial, reputational, operational, legal and regulatory, environmental, and people-related, or can result in the degradation of services. Often, there is a chain of consequence involved, and what begins as a people-related impact may develop into an operational one, leading for example to both financial and reputational impacts. It is important when conducting risk identification that these chains of consequence, illustrated in Figure 2.3, are not overlooked, since cumulatively, they can far exceed the originally identified impact.

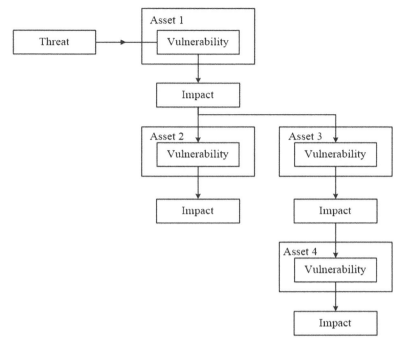

Figure 2.3 A chain of consequence

Impact or consequence can be stated in one of two ways—qualitatively, which is highly subjective, using descriptors such as "low," "medium," or "high"; or quantitatively, which is more objective, with numerically defined values such as $100,000 or 1,000 units per month.

Since the qualitative approach is often rather too subjective to permit an accurate risk assessment and the quantitative approach is usually much more complex and time-consuming, a half-way house is sometimes used, and this is known as semiquantitative assessment, in which bands of impact are given.

Table 2.1 illustrates how these semiquantitative assessments can be developed, and these are covered in greater detail in Chapter 4.

Vulnerabilities again are many and varied. Some will be so-called *intrinsic* vulnerabilities, which are present in all situations. For example, whether it is deliberately or accidentally applied, a strong magnetic field can erase the contents of a disc drive. Others will be so-called *extrinsic*

Table 2.1 Typical impact scales

Level of impact	Financial	Reputational	Legal and regulatory	Operational	Well-being
Very low	Losses of less than $100K	Negligible negative media coverage	Threat of possible action	Partial failure of one service	Little or no impact on staff
Low	Losses of between $100K and $500K	Some local negative media coverage	Penalties up to $10K	Total failure of one service	Minor loss of unskilled staff
Medium	Losses of between $500K and $1M	Some national negative media coverage	Penalties between $10K and $50K	Partial failure of multiple services	Major loss of unskilled staff
High	Losses of between $1M and $5M	Major national negative media coverage	Penalties between $50K and $100K	Total failure of multiple services	Minor loss of skilled staff
Very high	Losses in excess of $5M	Worldwide negative media coverage	Penalties in excess of $100K	Total failure of all services	Major loss of skilled staff

vulnerabilities, which are present when some action has either been taken or not taken, for example not changing a default password.

Vulnerabilities are covered in greater detail in Chapter 5.

There is some debate as to the order in which impacts, threats, or vulnerabilities should be assessed, but more importantly than the sequence of these is that they must all be carried out in order to complete the risk identification process.

Likelihood and *probability* represent the other half of the risk equation, and it is important to understand the difference between them. Likelihood is a qualitative term, and again is often highly subjective. We may characterize the likelihood of something happening as being low, medium, or high. Probability, on the other hand, is a quantitative or objective measure, and is often expressed in frequency terms such as a "once in ten years" event or in percentage terms such as a 20 percent chance that it will happen.

Table 2.2 Typical likelihood scales

Level of likelihood	External cyberattack	Internal cyberattack	System failures
Very low	Once a month	Once every 3 months	Once a year
Low	Once a week	Once a month	Once every 6 months
Medium	Multiple times a week	Multiple times a month	Once every 3 months
High	Once a day	Once a week	Once a month
Very high	Multiple times a day	Multiple times a week	Once a week

As with assessing impact or consequence, likelihood or probability can also be expressed in semiquantitative terms, as shown in Table 2.2. This allows some degree of flexibility while retaining defined boundaries for the assessment.

Finally, before the risk identification work commences, the means of approach—whether qualitative, quantitative, or semiquantitative—must be agreed, and in the case of the semiquantitative approach, what are the boundaries that define both impact and likelihood.

Next in the process of risk identification comes *risk analysis*. This involves plotting the risks we have identified on a risk matrix similar to that shown in Figure 2.4.

The values placed in each square of the matrix can be chosen in order to provide a form of weighting to the resulting analysis, where for example, the increase of impact from "trivial" to "minor" is considered to be of lesser importance than the increase from "possible" to "likely."

Using the above-mentioned matrix as an example, if a risk has been assessed as having a "major" impact and as being "likely" to occur, its value from the matrix would be rated as 20, and this will allow us to rank it against other risks of different ratings. When we move to the next stage, that of risk evaluation, this ranking will determine the priority in which we treat the risks. It is important to understand that the choice of five scales for each of impact and likelihood is arbitrary. Some organizations choose to use a greater number, affording more granularity; others choose

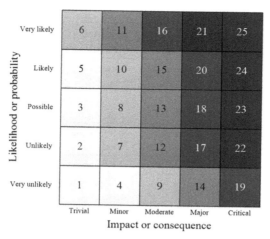

Figure 2.4 Example of a typical risk matrix

an even number of scales in order to avoid too many risks appearing in the middle ground.

Once plotted against the matrix, each risk can then be seen in the overall risk context, allowing the organization to deal more easily with the most urgent risks before those of lesser significance.

One final point on risk identification—if there is little or no impact or consequence, or if there is little of no likelihood or probability, then it follows that there is little or no risk. This does not mean we can ignore it completely though, as we shall see in the next section on risk treatment.

All risks should be recorded, and this is usually performed in a risk register that documents details of the threat, vulnerabilities, impacts or consequences, likelihood or probability, and the level of risk assessed. Once the risk evaluation process has been undertaken, the register may also contain details of how the risk is to be treated, by whom, and the proposed timescales.

Risk evaluation is the final stage in the risk assessment process, and offers the organization a number of choices of how to deal with the risk in question, and we shall deal with them in greater detail in Chapter 6.

At the highest or strategic level, there are four choices:

Avoid or *terminate* the risk. The organization may simply decide not to do whatever it is that would cause or allow the threat to materialize; for example, not to build a data center in a flood plain, not to install untested software, or not to allow a casual contractor to have root access to key operational systems!

Share or *transfer* the risk. This involves making a third party partly or even wholly responsible for dealing with the risk, although ownership of the risk must remain with the organization itself. This is usually carried out by some form of insurance, but the organization must be certain that any insurance policy has been thoroughly examined and approved by its legal department, since insurance companies will occasionally exploit a loophole in order to avoid paying out.

Reduce or *modify* the risk. While it is uncommon to be able to remove or reduce threats, it is much more usual (and often relatively straightforward) to reduce the likelihood or the probability that the threat will occur. This is often a simple action, such as maintaining the patch levels of operational software, thus avoiding unnecessary exploitation of a vulnerability, or by carrying out regular backups of business-critical data.

Risk reduction or modification sometimes does not completely reduce the level of risk to zero or near-zero levels, and a certain amount of so-called "residual" risk remains, which must be recorded and monitored on an ongoing basis.

Accept or *tolerate* the risk. When no other options are open, or if the level of risk is very low, then it can be accepted. However, it is important to understand that this does not mean that it can be ignored. Risks that are accepted must be reviewed periodically in order to ensure that the level of risk has not changed, which would require that the choice of avoid/terminate, share/transfer, reduce/modify must be taken again.

Risk Treatment

Once the strategic choice on how to deal with the risk has been made, we move to the tactical level. Here, there are four types of treatment:

- *Detective*, in which we use systems or human observers to discover when and where a cyber threat is being or has been carried out;

- *Directive*, in which we dictate actions that must be taken (and those that must not) in order to improve or maintain good cybersecurity;
- *Preventative*, in which we put measures into place that will prevent a cyber threat from being carried out or will reduce its impact;
- *Corrective*, in which we fix a problem that has occurred or is in the process of occurring as a result of a cyber threat being carried out.

Each of these tactical options will have one, two, or three operational choices:

- **Procedural measures.** These may be in the form of a statement in a policy document, for example a process that must be followed, or a work instruction that informs people how to go about undertaking some action.
- **Physical measures.** These usually involve some form of hardware, such as fences, gates, and entry control systems.
- **Technical measures.** These will include such areas as intrusion detection software and firewalls.

The choice of tactical or operational solution will depend greatly on the specific risk being addressed, and will often be agreed upon by a team of experts rather than by a single individual, and there is also the possibility that a risk may be addressed by more than one form of strategic, tactical, or operational approach, each making its own contribution to the overall treatment plan.

Communication and Consultation

It would be difficult (if almost impossible) for an individual to undertake a risk management activity alone. He or she would normally always require input from other areas of the organization in order to understand better how it works, what its deliverables are, and how disrupting events might affect these.

It will also be key to refer the individual risk assessments back to these sources in order to verify that all the input has been correctly recorded, interpreted, and assessed. Likewise, those other areas of the organization will be vital to helping develop the proposed solutions, and their input to that part of the process will often be essential in compiling business cases in order to obtain funding for the costlier work, especially if the funding must be procured by their departments.

Business Cases

It is worthwhile taking a brief look at the fundamentals of business cases, since these are generally the means by which we are able to obtain both capital and ongoing operational funds for the work the organization must undertake.

Unless you're lucky enough either to have an unlimited budget or a very understanding chief financial officer, you will certainly be obliged to make a formal request for the funds. There is usually a standard process for this in most organizations, and while this may vary in the detail from one organization to another, the decision-making panel will usually have certain general requirements.

You should be able to state the following:

What you want to spend the money on. This need not be a highly detailed list, but should include the key items, such as IT systems, software, network equipment, people, or outsourced services.

How much you plan to spend. This must cover both the capital items described earlier, and funds for specialist staff and contractors and also for ongoing regular service contracts such as maintenance upgrades and support.

When you will need to spend the money, so the finance department will know when to allocate funds.

The benefits of spending the money. This is often the most difficult area to cover, since there may be no obvious financial payback. Instead, you will need to focus more on the likely financial impact on the organization if a threat materializes. However, don't be too tempted to focus purely on the negative—senior executives are often wary of scare tactics and may feel they are being manipulated.

Since your work may be competing for funds with other (possibly revenue-generating) projects, you may find it advantageous to meet as many of the decision makers as possible before presenting your case and to briefly outline the project to them, allowing them the opportunity to ask questions and allowing you time to be able to research the answers, so that when it comes to the actual presentation, they are already familiar with the project and you will already have the answers to their key questions.

Most executives are busy people and dislike having to read through pages of technical data, so the material you present should begin with a one- or two-page executive summary that provides all the high-level information they need, but with any relevant background material behind it.

The presentation—if you are required to give one—should be brief and succinct. Ten minutes and ten slides should cover the points listed earlier. Always ask if they have any concerns or questions, and try to be sufficiently well prepared to be able to answer them on the spot. If not, be prepared to admit that you need time to find the answers, and tell them when you will be able to provide them.

Monitoring and Review

Clearly, once you have taken actions to treat a cybersecurity issue, you need to check whether or not the treatment has worked as expected. Whenever possible, the activity that delivers the treatment should include one or more tests to verify its effectiveness, and should allow for the treatment to be adjusted as necessary to make improvements. The results can be added to the risk register, allowing interested parties to see what has been achieved and how you have arrived there.

The fact that a risk has been treated, however, does not bring the matter to an end (unless the avoid or terminate route has been taken), as there will usually be some residual risk.

The risk should be reviewed—and if necessary the treatment should be retested—at agreed intervals to ensure both that the treatment is still delivering the expected results and that the level of risk has not changed.

If the organization has an internal audit function, it may wish to be included in such reviews, and in the case of extremely high-risk areas, may even insist on running the reviews itself.

Some people have a fear or distrust of internal audit, partly because they frequently bring more work as the result of reviews and partly because it brings about the feeling that you are not fully trusted. Involving them in projects to treat cyber risk may bring positive benefits, however, since their support when presenting business cases can easily swing the decision in your favor.

Summary

In this chapter, we have reviewed the basic principles of risk management and explored the terminology used. In the next chapter, we will examine the next stage—that of establishing the context of the organization and understanding its information assets, which represents the first part of the overall risk management and business continuity process.

CHAPTER 3

The Main Cybersecurity Issues

In February 2018, the US Government published a report[1] that suggested that the cost to the U.S. economy in 2016 from malicious cyber activity was somewhere between $57 billion and $109 billion. On the basis of any one of the financial estimates of the International Monetary Fund, World Bank, or United Nations, this is greater in monetary terms than the Global Domestic Product of more than 110 countries. The report does not even address the malicious cyber activity that took place in 2017, or in the years before, and it is just for the United States. The financial problem alone then is massive, and does not scratch the surface of the other issues that contribute to this, or are further affected by it.

In this chapter, we shall describe the main cybersecurity issues that affect organizations and create business continuity challenges.

At first sight, some of these issues may not appear to be relevant to business continuity, but as we shall see later, the resulting impacts can be truly business-affecting, since as we saw in Chapter 2, there is often a chain of consequence between the original threat being carried out and the final result. Typically, cybersecurity issues tend to fall into one of five categories, and we'll review each in turn:

- **Cybercrime**. In this section, I refer to what I call "mainstream" cybercrime, such as theft, website defacement, denial of service attacks, and the like. Some topics, although they may constitute cybercrime offences, warrant a section of their own.

---

[1]See https://www.whitehouse.gov/wp-content/uploads/2018/02/The-Cost-of-Malicious-Cyber-Activity-to-the-U.S.-Economy.pdf

- **Cyber bullying or harassment.** I have separated this quite deliberately, since not only does it differ in many respects from other types of cybercrime, but also can be a precursor to them, as we shall see later.
- **Cyber warfare.** As unlikely as it might at first appear, cyber warfare can have a dramatic impact on all kinds of organization—not only on the military forces themselves, but also on those organizations that supply or provide supporting services to the military and, when applied as a political weapon as opposed to a purely military one, will have a much wider impact.
- **Cyber surveillance.** On one side of the cyber surveillance coin, the section examines the personal privacy aspects of life in a cyberworld. On the other side, it deals with the state surveillance of individuals and organizations who for whatever reason come to the attention of the authorities.
- **Cybersecurity failures.** Technical security problems will always arise, whether through failures of hardware, software, or system configuration. The challenge is for organizations to be able to respond quickly to such incidents and either to fix them or to find a suitable work-around until such time as a complete solution can be found.

The first issue we shall consider is the one having the greatest financial impact on both individuals and organizations alike—that of cybercrime.

Cybercrime

The definition of cybercrime varies somewhat from one jurisdiction to another, but generally refers to the action or actions taken by an attacker aimed at stealing from or disrupting the operation of an individual's or an organization's information technology (IT) systems and services. However, since this type of crime is frequently the enabler by which more conventional crimes (theft, blackmail, extortion, etc.) are carried out, the definitions do not always include these aspects as well.

In September 2017, the credit report organization Equifax revealed that it had suffered a cybersecurity breach that exploited a website vulnerability earlier in the year, and which potentially affected more than 140 million customers in the United States, United Kingdom, and Canada. Details including social security numbers, dates of birth, and addresses were stolen, and also the credit card details of at least 200,000 customers. The company later estimated that the costs of the attack could eventually exceed $100 million.[2]

Broadly speaking, cybercrime breaks down into a number of well-defined areas:

- Financial theft
- Website defacement
- Exploitation
- Denial of Service (DoS) attacks
- Copyright violation
- Intellectual Property (IP) theft
- The use of dark patterns[3]

Some of these areas require a prior action (criminal or otherwise) to have taken place. For example, if an attacker is able to withdraw cash from your bank account, he or she can have done so only by having stolen or guessed your security credentials. Guessing them is not in itself a criminal act, although making use of them is, whereas stealing the credentials is an offence in its own right.

In the context of business continuity, any or all of these can result in a negative impact on an organization.

Financial theft tends to be the first type of cybercrime that we think of since it generally has both the greatest impact and the most media coverage. However, in those situations where someone's credentials have previously been acquired, the impact can reach much further. Identity theft is on the rise, and although we may think of this as purely affecting individuals, we should remember that the theft of a chief financial officer's work credentials could result in highly serious consequences.

---

[2]See https://www.nytimes.com/2017/09/07/business/equifax-cyberattack.html

[3]The use of dark patterns is not in itself a crime, but is often intended to entrap the unwitting user into being a victim of crime, or at least a "legal" scam.

Financial theft is not only about stealing money or other financial instruments—it can also relate to IP theft such as industrial processes, designs, photographs, video media, music, and pharmaceutical formulae.

Website defacement is a very common form of cybercrime—usually resulting only in reputational damage to the organization. However, when this is the result of a revenge attack for some actual or perceived injustice, the defacement can either be blatant, for example promoting homophobic, racial, or religious hatred; or more insidious, in which links on the website take people to webpages they might normally avoid such as those containing more extreme or unsavory content, or to locations containing malware or those that conduct phishing attacks to garner user credentials.

Exploitation often involves the theft of such assets as an organization's customer database that contains financial credentials, resulting not only in the customers being the subject of financial theft, but also the organization suffering substantial embarrassment and reputational consequences if and when knowledge of the loss became public. Some organizations that have been impacted by exploitation attacks choose to keep the fact a secret, but when the details do become known, the reputational damage can be much greater. However, it should be said that if handled correctly, the organization's reputational damage can be minimized, and can even recover.

For example, in late 2017, the taxi firm Uber was discovered to have covered up a successful cyberattack for a whole year and which had resulted in the details of 57 million customers being stolen.[4] Unsurprisingly, their chief security officer was fired when it became clear that the information was stored in an unencrypted form. Fortunately for their customers, Uber had paid the attackers $100,000 to delete the data they had stolen and to maintain silence. At least, it is to be hoped that the attackers kept their part of the bargain! Unfortunately for Uber, this does not appear to have improved their reputation in the slightest!

There are several lessons to be learned here, and we shall cover these on the section on communication in Chapter 7.

---

[4]https://www.theguardian.com/technology/2017/nov/21/uber-data-hack-cyber-attack

Denial of Service (DoS) and Distributed Denial of Service (DDoS) Attacks

DoS and DDoS attacks are designed either to slow down or to prevent access to an organization's website and back-end services. There are a number of techniques used to achieve this, but in general it involves flooding the website with false or an excessive number of connection requests, so that it spends enormous amounts of system resources in responding to them, making it extremely difficult if not impossible for the website to respond to valid requests.

For many organizations, the results of this could be catastrophic, since those that do business entirely online—for example amazon or eBay—would either have their operations seriously degraded or be completely unable to trade and those who provide a public service would have their operations severely curtailed—for example those governmental organizations providing online services such as social service enquiries. These organizations would probably be contactable by telephone, but their lines would become quickly overwhelmed.

DoS and DDoS attacks are frequently used in response to a perceived injustice, whether real or imaginary, and can also be mounted in conjunction with a demand for some form of ransom or forfeit to be paid.

Intellectual Property (IP) Theft

IP is sometimes seen as a catchall for a number of areas, including trademarks, patents, and copyright. As copyright is often considered to be a special case; I have described that separately in the following paragraphs.

Trademarks don't just include such features as names and logos, but can also include phrases that link back to the organization's brand. Many large corporations successfully sue much smaller companies for trademark infringement, even if the link between them is tenuous, knowing that the smaller organization will have much fewer financial resources with which to fight back. However, the tide may be turning here, when fans of the smaller organization use crowdsourcing to generate funds to fight the case and at the same time cause embarrassment to the larger organization for attacking "the little guy."

Patent infringement is even bigger business, especially in the United States, where high-tech companies develop small components (both hardware and software) that are later used in products by other organizations. A good example of this is that of a federal case in which Apple was fined more than $500 million, having been judged to have infringed three of the patents of Smartflash, a Texas-based company that developed software providing access to payment systems, digital rights management, and data storage, all of which Apple used in its iTunes software.

Sometimes, however, it is impossible for the victim to gain redress against an attacker, as in the case of Lockheed-Martin, whose designs for the F-35 fighter jet were allegedly stolen by attackers sponsored by the Chinese government.

Copyright Violation

Copyright is generally applicable to the field of creativity such as literary, musical, or artistic work. Copyright violation is frequently but not always carried out with financial gain in mind. Violating another person's or an organization's copyright may deprive them of income in the form of royalties, or alternatively it may provide the violator with royalty income for something that has not been written or developed by them. For example, in 2016, the rock group Led Zeppelin finally settled a long-standing dispute for allegedly violating the copyright of Spirit's 1967 song Taurus in their 1971 Stairway to Heaven, when the jury eventually decided in favor of Led Zeppelin. However, the point here is that not only did one party feel deprived of their copyright while the other gained significantly, but also a huge amount of money was spent over the years in legal fees!

A similar example is the case in which on this occasion the victim was successful was in connection with The Hollies' 1974 hit The Air That I Breathe, which was accepted as being plagiarized by Radiohead's 1992 recording Creep. In a bizarre twist at the time of writing, Radiohead is in dispute with Lana Del Ray over her current recording Get Free, comparing it with Creep.

Dark Patterns

As mentioned earlier in this chapter, dark patterns, while not actually a crime, are generally unethical methods used by website developers to encourage users to make a choice or selection they might not make normally make. Sometimes the text on web pages will be unclear, and you will find that you have unintentionally agreed to download software or accept an offer.

Organizations can make use of psychological analysis to identify the shapes, sizes, locations on the web page and colors of buttons, click boxes, and text best suited to user selection—and those that they are less likely to be used—when accessing web pages. The result of this is that users are encouraged to select the organization's choice rather than their own.

At other times, items you did not request might be added to your shopping basket, and if you aren't sufficiently careful or use the one click method of purchase, you may discover that you have inadvertently purchased something you didn't want as well as the items that you did.

This process is referred to as a dark patterning, and the extremely subtle techniques employed rely on well-understood aspects of human behavior.

You may, for example, while booking an airline seat, find that the airline has included the offer of travel insurance. If you are a frequent traveler, you will doubtless already have this, but if you miss the opportunity to remove it when checking out, you may discover either that you have bought it and may experience difficulty in obtaining a refund, or that it is extremely challenging subsequently to opt out of buying it as the option will be hidden from view.

Now while there is nothing technically illegal about these dark patterns, they do represent sharp practice, especially where it increases that website organization's revenue at the expense of the consumer.

Cyber Harassment

Although cyber harassment does not directly cause issues for the cyber infrastructure in organizations, it can be used to cause staff to carry out actions they would otherwise avoid. Cyber harassment can take several different forms—some can be extremely distressing to individual employees, delivering abuse, threatening physical violence, or threatening to reveal personal information that they would rather did not become public knowledge. These often originate from a person or persons known to the victim. Other forms of harassment can be more subtle—for example, repetitive text messages or e-mails suggesting that the victim has won a competition; or that there is a delivery waiting for him or her. This variety may well contain some form of link to a website containing malware which will affect the victim's computer or connect to a phishing site that will lure the victim into parting with personal or company information.

Occasionally, however, the two forms can be combined in situations where the attacker wishes to gain access to sensitive information regarding the organization itself or perhaps one of its senior managers and applies pressure to the victim in order to achieve this. On other occasions, the victim will be an unwitting participant by simply clicking on an e-mail link, allowing malware to enter the organization's IT systems.

In many countries, cyber harassment is now considered to be a crime, and in cases where the attacker is known to the victim, successful prosecution may result. However, when the identity of the attacker is either unknown or less obvious, it will be much more difficult to use legal means to obtain redress.

Cyber Warfare

Warfare is generally thought of as being related to action that takes place between nation-states, sometimes referred to as symmetric warfare because they are usually relatively evenly matched in terms of capability. On other occasions, the exchange takes place between terrorist organizations and nation-states, and this is sometimes referred to as asymmetric warfare since terrorist groups tend to be much smaller than nation-states, but can still inflict significant damage.

Cyber warfare is no different in this respect; two large nation-states—for example both the United States and Russia—have the resources to carry out cyberattacks against each other, but so do much smaller organizations with significantly fewer resources, since a large physical presence is not a major criterion, while technical know-how and capability combined with sufficient motivation can deliver devastating results. Such organizations are less easy to locate, often relying on loosely knit cells of like-minded individuals rather than centrally grouped forces.

While the targets here are normally the military or economic resources of the "victim" nation, there is frequently collateral damage to other organizations within that nation. A classic example of this is that mentioned earlier of the cyberattack against Lockheed-Martin in which designs for the F-35 fighter jet were stolen, allowing an enemy nation (attributed to China) to be able to develop, build, and potentially sell fighters of the same capability.

There are issues further downstream as well, since suppliers to organizations like Lockheed-Martin would also potentially suffer in a chain of consequence as a result of the attack.

Cyber Surveillance

Cyber surveillance also might not appear to be an issue for business continuity in organizations, but in reality, it can be a precursor to future cybercrime. Criminals who want to target an individual or an organization may take considerable time and efforts in monitoring the activities of key individuals, so that they can be exploited in one way or another. Typically, this will either be in order to access the individual or organization's information or credentials with the objective of stealing money or IP, or to gain access to systems with the intention of holding the individual or organization to ransom.

Cyber surveillance may either be targeted at key individuals, especially board members or senior staff, or may be a more general "catchall" surveillance, in which a picture of the organization is built up partly from publicly available information and partly from more intrusive investigations.

Whichever type of surveillance is used, the final result will inevitably be some form of damage to the individual or to the organization.

Cybersecurity Failures

Security weaknesses are often present, hidden deep within an organization's IT systems. In January 2018, it was announced that two security flaws, known as Meltdown and Spectre, had been discovered. Both of these can affect the main Windows, Mac OS, and Unix computing platforms, and the problem stems from a weakness in the design of the central processing unit which chip manufacturers are responsible for creating. Those organizations that produce the operating systems that use these chips have been busy developing patches to rectify the problem, and the chip manufacturers have been developing new versions of the chips with the problem removed. At the time of announcement, it was clear that the vulnerability had not actually been exploited, but it does beg the question not as to whether there could be other hidden flaws both in the hardware or the operating systems that have not yet come to light, but how many.

That aside, there are other security failures that can cause serious issues. Some of these will be in the incorrect configuration of IT systems and services, while others will be caused by incorrect or inappropriate use of them.

Again, either way, business continuity issues can and will arise through security failures such as these.

Summary

This chapter has described the high-level cybersecurity issues that can and do result in business continuity challenges for organizations of all kinds and sizes as well as individual users.

We shall go into greater detail about the threats and vulnerabilities that cause these in a later chapter, but next we shall examine the various information assets that organizations operate, and the impacts that are likely to result from a cybersecurity breach.

CHAPTER 4

Information Assets and Impacts

The organization's information-related assets together with the systems and networks that underpin them are key to the ongoing ability of all organizations to operate successfully, and therefore a detailed understanding of these assets is required in order to carry out a risk assessment prior to introducing measures to prevent or reduce cybersecurity-related business continuity problems. This chapter will describe how an organization may identify these and make a meaningful estimate of their value to the business.

All of these assets can be negatively impacted by cybersecurity issues in one form or another, so we shall then examine the kinds of impact that are likely to arise if the assets are attacked in some way.

We tend to use the terms "data" and "information" in the same context, but in fact they are slightly different as we shall see.

Information Assets

We may tend to think of information assets as being restricted to files and documents stored on computer systems, and while this is some way from the reality, the view represents an excellent starting point for this section. Before we do that, let's take a closer look at information and how it is actually part of a hierarchy.

The Journey of Data

We begin by gathering data—small items that may have some meaning on their own, but which when added to other data elements begin to tell

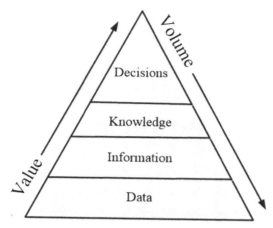

Figure 4.1 The information hierarchy

us more about the subject. For example, take my name. I never thought it was a particularly common name until I began researching my family history and discovered that there are actually quite a number of people with the same name around the world. If you add my date of birth, you reduce the number to much more manageable levels, but you still don't have sufficient information to pinpoint me. However, if you add an address, a telephone number, or a social security number, you can probably pinpoint me very quickly. Combining or aggregating the appropriate data elements provides information, and this is especially powerful when it is collected for large numbers of individuals (often referred to as "big data"), and can be used in a number of ways—either in a benign fashion, in which the information is used to understand the bigger picture, as in the case of the national census—or for more commercial purposes such as marketing. The information hierarchy is shown in Figure 4.1.

As we move further up the hierarchy, combining large amounts of information allows the extraction or generation of knowledge, which can ultimately lead to an ability to make decisions, predictions, or deductions. Generally, as we move up the hierarchy the value increases, while the volume decreases. It follows, therefore, that as an organization's information assets become more refined, their value to the organization increases dramatically.

Once we have information, it is only an asset to the organization if it has some use or purpose, and needs to be handled in a formal way. Figure 4.2 illustrates the information lifecycle.

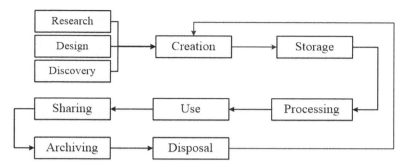

Figure 4.2 The information lifecycle

The information lifecycle process begins with some kind of development, research, design, or discovery, which allows the organization to record the information in some form, whether in electronic or hard copy form, and then to store it in some way. Nowadays, even original documents that are paper-based are scanned in and stored on computers, since organizations find that they are easier to manage it in this way.

Information is usually then processed by some means, either by reformatting it in a way that makes it more accessible or by enriching it in some way. An example of this is taking documents of any kind and reformatting them into the Adobe Acrobat portable document format (pdf), which is universally accessible from all types of computer operating systems and mobile computing platforms.

The process then continues with use either by the organization itself or by others whether individually or collaboratively, at which point it can be shared either within or outside the organization, depending upon its purpose.

As time progresses, the information may become out of date but may either still have some residual value or possess legal constraints which preclude its destruction, in which case it may be archived. Finally, the information will have become completely redundant, and depending on retention requirements may be safely disposed of or destroyed. Alternatively, it may be updated and reused when combined with new or updated information.

At each stage of the information life cycle, it will be necessary to ensure that the information is adequately protected from accidental or deliberate alteration or loss.

Information can be bought and sold, and the sharing of information—especially personal information—can be very controversial. In many countries, there is legislation that restricts how and when such information can be acquired, stored, used, shared, and eventually destroyed, and is frequently the misuse or abuse of large quantities of personal information that causes business continuity issues for organizations that do not take cybersecurity as seriously as they should.

Take the example of the Ashley Madison dating service. In 2015, their website was breached by a group of hackers known as The Impact Team who stole almost 100 gigabytes of sensitive personal data including names, addresses, and credit card details covering the records of 37 million users. Some or all of these records were placed on the Internet, and news of the leak became public knowledge. Ultimately, the company paid more than $11 million to its users in compensation. We shall look further at the impact of this kind of action later in this chapter.

Information and Intellectual Property (IP)

It is often said that information is the life blood of any organization, and as such it is sometimes taken for granted—until it is either missing, unavailable, or incorrect. Without access to accurate passenger and flight details, no airline can operate its services—passengers cannot check in, flight deck and cabin crew cannot be scheduled, cargo cannot be loaded, fuel and catering supplies cannot be delivered.

Information can come in many forms, some of which are easy to overlook. These include such things as the following:

Financial statements	Configuration data
Audio files	Video files
Software	Website data
Measurements	Social media records
Formulae	Text messages and e-mails
Picture files	Digital signatures
Payment details	Office documents
Processes and procedures	Database records

You may be able to think of many more, but the aforementioned list illustrates the range of information that an organization might require in order to conduct its day-to-day affairs.

Some of this information will be normal "business" information, whereas other information will be more commercially sensitive, especially if it relates to designs, patents, recipes, and formulae on which the organization's business is based. This is normally referred to as intellectual property (IP), is often acquired after considerable time, cost and effort, and in certain circumstances can make or break a business. Organizations generally take great care in protecting their IP, especially from blatant copying—just try using an icon of an apple with a bite taken from its right-hand side in a company logo and you'll see what I mean—as well as use of another organization's IP without its prior approval or some form of licensing agreement.

IP also extends to the copyright of other creative media. When writing, I have occasionally used extracts from the standards of the International Standards Organisation in the text, and part of my duty as an author is ensuring that I have the appropriate permissions to use these before the book goes into the publishing process.

Staff

I have heard organizations make the statement "People are our greatest asset" many times. Sometimes they even mean it, but the reality is that when they are looking at the cybersecurity arrangements, staff (apart from specialist security staff) don't always figure in the thinking. This is indefensible. Many cybersecurity issues are caused by staff who are either incorrectly trained or who aren't made aware of the risks. Staff can be both the first line and the last line of cyber defense, and should always be considered as a major part of the overall process when the organization conducts its impact assessments, and subsequently puts controls in place to mitigate the risks.

Processes

As with staff, processes, procedures, guidelines, and work instructions are also organizational assets that are frequently overlooked. They inform staff in all areas of the organization what they must (or must not) do in any given situation and just as importantly how they should do it. If processes are ignored or by-passed, bad things can and will happen.

Take as an example a new computer system that is introduced. Apart from loading its operating system and applications, its security configuration will require careful setting up. One of the key functions of this part of the process will be to change the default or root passwords, but it is incredible how often this is either accidentally or deliberately overlooked by the team responsible.

Equally important is that all these processes should be fully documented, and should follow the information life cycle described earlier in this chapter.

Technology

After information and IP itself, technology—Information Technology (IT) systems, network equipment, firewalls, and the like are the assets that most organizations consider to be of the highest value to the organization—not only because of the often high initial capital cost, but also because they are the means by which all the organization's information is stored. Also, communication links form an integral part of the technology asset base, since without these the organization will effectively stand isolated from its suppliers and customers alike.

However, many organizations nowadays are allowing staff to use their own computers and smartphones as a business tool, and although these are not actually a company-owned asset, in the overall scheme of things they should be considered along with everything that is, since they may contain information that is vital to, or potentially damaging to, the organization's continuing operations.

Physical Environment

The physical environment in which the organization operates is also a major asset—buildings in particular and the infrastructure within them that support the organization's operations are fundamental in business continuity terms. Computer rooms, along with their power supplies, air-conditioning, and support services, must be included when considering the environment in which both technology and people work.

Supply Chain

The organization's supply chain is another business-critical asset—again one that is easily overlooked in cybersecurity terms, since although a supplier's security issues are for them to solve and not the organization itself, these issues can rapidly escalate into issues for the organization being supplied with consequential impacts on their customers. It is, therefore, incumbent upon organizations that have a business-critical supply chain to ensure that all aspects of this are protected.

Supply chain considerations can also include third-party organizations that provide a service to the organization—not only services directly related to IT systems, but also any support services that underpin the organization's business-critical operations—for example power supply or maintenance of environmental systems.

Cloud Services

Cloud service providers can also be considered to be an element in the supply chain, but they are generally much more than this, since they may not only provide storage of business-critical information, but may also operate and manage the IT platforms upon which much of the organization's operations are conducted. This puts cloud service provision at the very heart of the organization, and may raise its importance far beyond that of other organizations in the supply chain.

Security requirements are occasionally overlooked when choosing a cloud service provider, since reducing costs is normally the main driving force for this activity. Even worse, the ability to withdraw cleanly from a cloud service contract may have been overlooked by the contract negotiators.

An organization I am aware of found itself in exactly this position, and although it was able to recover all its information, the negotiating team had not considered the index to all their information which had been generated subsequently by the cloud service provider, and they were forced to purchase this at an extortionate cost.

Impacts

Let's now turn to the impacts or consequences that a cybersecurity incident might cause in terms of business continuity. As we have already said, many of these will be financial impacts in one way or another, since this is generally where either a single impact or a chain of consequence will end.

Typically, impacts or consequences fall into one of five general categories, and we shall expand a little on each:

- Financial
- Reputation
- Legal and regulatory
- Operational
- Well-being of people

Financial Impacts

The financial impacts that will be felt most immediately will be those that result from the curtailment of current business. If the organization's ability to process existing orders, to produce the goods or services, or to take new orders are stopped or seriously reduced in capability, cash flow will soon be reduced. Since many organizations make use of the flow of cash to finance future development and production, this would be a serious problem.

If business-impacting cyber incidents were to become public knowledge, then customers may decide to cancel or curtail contracts, and the organization might find that the cost of borrowing (to provide a financial buffer while regaining control) might also increase.

Some organizations might discover that their inability to supply contractually agreed goods or services could result in penalties being imposed—not something that any organization needs when it is already facing financial difficulties.

Then there are the costs of repairing the damage—potentially both for staff and systems, and in the case where key information has been lost, there are also the costs of recovery, redevelopment, or replacement.

For those organizations listed on the national or international stock exchanges, once cybersecurity issues become public knowledge, there

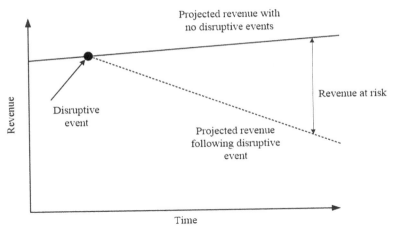

Figure 4.3 Financial loss projection

would undoubtedly be an immediate drop in the organization's stock or share value, although for those organizations that take steps to resolve the problems quickly and effectively, this might recover with time, as has been seen in a number of cases. However, as a consequence, the organization might find that insurance premiums—especially those covering cyber-related issues have increased considerably in cost.

If the disruptive event is not brought under control, the financial impacts will increase and grow with time, as shown in Figure 4.3.

Reputational Impacts

Reputations are like eggs, they are easily broken and almost impossible to reassemble!

Reputational damage is almost always highly detrimental to any organization, whether in the public or private sector, since most organizations trade heavily on their reputation.

In order to ensure their reputation remains high, many organizations employ dedicated specialists who are skilled in placing a positive spin on bad news with the objective of countering negative publicity. It is typical that in such organizations, staff are strongly advised (and often actually instructed) against talking directly to the press, but always to divert enquiries to the corporate communication department. This is especially important in situations where highly sensitive or confidential information has made its way into the public domain.

Reputational impacts invariably include loss of confidence on the national and international stock markets, with the consequent reduction in company value, leading to a negative perception by customers, other organizations in the sector and the general public alike, and also to possible takeover by a predatory competitor. At the same time, an organization's competitors will often be quick to take advantage of the situation and tempt customers away from the affected organization, sometimes never to return.

When an organization is already in dire straits as a result of a major incident, the last thing it needs is to be stricken with further financial implications, which is why it will (or at least should) take great care of its reputation.

Legal and Regulatory Impacts

Like in the case of reputational impacts, legal and regulatory impacts can have serious repercussions on any organization, and dealing with these is ideally handled by legal specialists within the organization or contracted in from specialist companies.

Legal and regulatory impacts will occasionally include warnings for first-time "offences," or more generally will result in penalties from government or sector regulators, especially in the financial and health sectors.

Organizations that are unable to file their company accounts on time may suffer fines for late submission or for late payment of taxes, while those whose services are curtailed may be the subject of damages for breaches of contract.

Most of the above-mentioned impacts have a consequential financial impact—remember those chains of consequence we talked about earlier?

In cases where cybersecurity issues have been caused by fraud or other criminal acts, the potential consequences could be very severe, and might even result in custodial sentences for senior officers of the organization.

Operational Impacts

Operational impacts are invariably recognized much more quickly. Most of these will be very obvious, as in the example of staff being unable to access information they require in order to complete their tasks, or which they can see is fundamentally incorrect.

On most occasions, operational impacts will result in subsequent financial impacts, and the inability to comply with a service contract may well result in claims for contractual damages, or at best lost orders for further contracts.

Operational impacts that occur as the result of a cybersecurity incident invariably include the loss of or damage to information (confidentiality, integrity, and availability), and in the very worst case may have caused serious damage to the IT infrastructure, requiring major rebuild and reconfiguration work. Naturally, there will be significant costs associated with this work coupled with the loss of revenue while the problems are corrected, often far exceeding the costs of appropriate preventative measures.

While the organization is in the process of recovering from a cybersecurity incident, it will have a reduced ability to be competitive or to progress new business or product or service developments. This can be highly damaging, both in the short term and in the longer term, especially where speed to market and so-called "agile" development is key to the organization's business strategy.

Third-party relations will also suffer damage when operational impacts occur. Organizations may find themselves in the position of stalling or canceling deliveries, and where outsourced contracts are involved in product or service provision, these too may have to be placed on hold, and the supplier may be forced to lay off staff as a result. There's that chain of consequence at work again!

Finally, the organization's management may find that while fire-fighting the cybersecurity incident, it has much reduced ability to maintain control of the remainder of the organization's operations. It is usually for this reason that some organizations adopt a two- or three-tier approach to incident management, as we shall see later.

Impacts on the Well-being of People

When a major cybersecurity incident arises, the organization's staff will typically be split into three distinct groups—those who are overseeing management of the incident (normally senior managers), those who are actually dealing with the issue itself (normally technical staff), and everybody else.

The first two groups will undoubtedly be suffering some form of stress or trauma as they deal with the problem at whatever level. As for everybody else, it may be the case that all they can do is sit and wait for the problem to be resolved before they can continue with their work. In the worst case, they may have to be laid off temporarily until such time as they are needed again, and this will inevitably have an adverse effect on the entire organization's staff by lowering their morale. It is in circumstances such as these that staff who might otherwise be happy to stay with the organization will decide to leave, and if enough do so, especially enough key staff, the consequential effect on the organization will be even worse.

Summary

In this chapter, we have examined the kinds of assets that can be impacted by a cybersecurity incident, and the kinds of impact that can result. In the next chapter, we shall move on to discuss the vulnerabilities that these assets may exhibit, and the threats that can cause the impacts.

CHAPTER 5

Vulnerabilities and Threats

Now that we've covered some of the theory and understood the issues at stake, the types of asset that can be affected, together with the possible impacts, we can continue by examining the vulnerabilities that can permit many of these threats to occur, and then move on to the main threats that can be the cause of cyber issues.

Business Continuity Cyber Vulnerabilities

Vulnerabilities are weaknesses in assets that can be exploited by threats. Typical examples would be little or no access control in computer systems, or poor physical security at the organization's buildings.

It is not unreasonable to imagine that most vulnerabilities are of a technical nature, but this is actually far from correct. It is true that many vulnerabilities are technical, and many are solved by applying technical solutions. However, there are other types of vulnerability that can allow cyber threats to be successful, such as processes and people-related vulnerabilities.

Every time a vulnerability is identified, there may be additional data available regarding whether the vulnerability is known to have been successfully exploited, and whether there might be known controls are already available that will permit some degree of mitigation of the vulnerability, either fully or in part.

Even the most thorough risk assessment might not identify every vulnerability that could affect the organization, and since new vulnerabilities will emerge over time, vulnerability assessment should be revisited regularly.

Let's now consider the various types of vulnerability that we may experience. From a cyber perspective, these tend to fall into one of five distinct areas:

- Access control failures
- Systems acquisition, development, and maintenance procedures
- Physical and environmental failures
- Operational management failures
- People-related security failures

Access Control Failures

Access control is used both to permit access to information resources for persons who are authorized and to deny access to persons who are not authorized to access those resources. Access control failures are one of the main means by which successful cyberattacks take place.

There are two general areas where access control failures occur. The first is the failure to change users' access rights when they are changing their role within the organization, and especially the failure to revoke all access rights when users leave the organization. Additionally, there is a widespread failure to restrict the use of system utilities, which can allow users themselves to change the configuration of their computers, potentially reducing the strength of the security settings.

The second area is that of failures in user password management, in which users are allowed to use easily guessed passwords; in which the default accounts and passwords of systems are not changed; and where the use of embedded passwords in software applications is permitted.

Systems Acquisition, Development, and Maintenance Procedures

At one time or another, all organizations update older systems and software, acquire new ones, and also develop new software applications. It is essential that selection and development is carried out in a formal and controlled manner and that criteria which include appropriate security features are considered. Rigorous analysis and testing of new software is required in order to discover whether or not it contains known vulnerabilities (it often does), and these kinds of vulnerability frequently go unnoticed until they result in serious consequences later on. The root cause of this is often as the direct result of a desire to achieve cost savings.

In order to avoid these kinds of vulnerabilities, the organization should define and adhere to clear functional purchasing and development specifications, avoiding the use of untested and unauthorized software.

Another cause of vulnerabilities is the failure to validate data entry, such as entries that exceed a defined number of characters, resulting in application software failing, often into an unpredictable state, and allowing buffer overflow attacks to be successful.

One of the most critical errors is the failure of organizations to plan for the disaster recovery of business-critical systems. We shall deal with this area in much greater detail in Chapter 7.

Physical and Environmental Failures

Physical security defects are normally highly visible, not only to staff but also to potential intruders, allowing them to gain access to an organization's buildings and ultimately their systems with the result that a local cyberattack can take place as opposed to a remote attack. The presence of robust security measures is generally sufficient to deter intruders, but it is vital that these measures are well maintained.

Such measures include controlled access to premises, especially to sensitive areas such as equipment rooms and cabling closets, and particularly with regard to doors and windows.

Environmental vulnerabilities that result in cyber-related issues tend to arise from the environmental subsystems that underpin major premises such as power supplies, cooling, and humidity control systems. Imagine the consequences of remotely shutting down the air-conditioning plant at a major data center.

Operational Management Failures

Failures of operations management provide endless opportunity for vulnerabilities to be successfully exploited, whether these are deliberate or accidental. Underpinning operational management failures are almost always issues with policies and procedures—either through the failure of users and security staff to observe them or the failure of the organization to produce them in the first instance.

Operations management failures include the failure to ensure that the appropriate segregation of duties is observed, especially where security staff can change the access permissions of users, the absence of audit trails, things that ensure that anomalies can be identified easily, and the segregation of test and production systems.

Failure to ensure robust network monitoring including intrusion detection can result in users bypassing security systems by installing their own wireless access points in order to gain unauthorized access both to internal networks and to unprotected public networks. This kind of operational failure also includes the need for formal Bring Your Own Device policies.

Another area in which operational management failures occur is in the failure to keep malware protection up-to-date, in patching of operating system and application software, and in operational change management procedures, all of which can result in successful cyberattacks, taking advantage of vulnerabilities in older versions of software and in more recently introduced malware.

People-Related Security Failures

People-related security failures are caused by mistakes or oversights by the organization's users and operational staff. They are mostly related to policies, processes, and procedures that require them to follow prescribed instructions, such as avoiding selecting attachments in unsolicited e-mails or in the case of unsupervised work by third-party organizations or by staff who work outside normal business hours.

However, other types of people-related security failures are the result of deliberate actions by demotivated or disgruntled staff who seek to disrupt the organization's business activities by causing damage for a real or perceived injustice of some kind. This can include such things as deleting or changing information, or copying sensitive company information and selling it to other interested parties—competitors for instance.

We should not overlook actions by staff who have been deliberately infiltrated within the organization in order to steal the organization's IP, and this aspect of operational failures must be linked to the organization's human resources policies regarding verification of the credentials of job applicants.

Data Stripping

When an organization develops its public-facing website, it is extremely common to update the contents at regular intervals—often many times daily. When new information is placed on the website, one aspect that is frequently overlooked is that of the metadata that accompanies the information itself.

An innocuous document can easily contain information that identifies the name of an employee, his or her internal username, versions of software used to produce the website information, dates, times, and locations of photographic images, and the network names of computer systems used in the organization. All of these can easily be recovered automatically by an attacker, using a technique known as "scraping."

Having acquired this metadata, the attacker would then begin to target the users via social media or e-mails to their work address, and would try to exploit known vulnerabilities in the software of systems on the organization's network.

When developing or updating their website, the organization should always ensure that this metadata is stripped out of any documents before they are and placed online.

The Internet of Things (IoT)

The IoT, in which almost anything that can be internet-connected, and can be accessed from anywhere, is firmly with us. Light bulbs, central heating thermostats, white goods, door locks, and children's toys are just a few of the many household items that can be part of the IoT, which, therefore, deserves a section all to itself, since it—or at least the things that combine to make it—represent real potential for cyber vulnerabilities. Indeed, many have already been discovered.

The so-called top ten IoT issues listed in a report[1] by the Infosec Institute give us some idea of the range of issues that the IoT may bring us.

---

[1] See resources.infosecinstitute.com/the-top-ten-iot-vulnerabilities

The main item on the list is that of the so-called "shaky web interface"—the means by which the device is controlled by an application—whether on a computer or smartphone. Many of these are poorly written, and either do not function as they should or worse still leak personal data. While this is just one of the 10 issues on the list, it has ramifications across the board. The applications that are used to access it may also exhibit poor performance or security weaknesses, and in some cases may not have any security at all. Even when they do, the security aspects of the device may be basic at best, and may allow the user to turn them off completely.

Not least of the issues are those affecting so-called "intelligent personal assistants" (IPAs). These come in a variety of forms—some as an application on smartphones such as Apple's Siri or Microsoft's Cortana, or built into a hardware platform such as Amazon's Echo/Alexa system, Apple's Homekit or Microsoft's Xbox.

These IPAs respond to the human voice and will undertake a variety of actions when triggered. In most cases, they will simply attempt to turn the voice command into an Internet search, but if a connection has been made with another IoT device, they can also to cause it to undertake some action, for example to turn a light on or off or to adjust the room temperature. In early 2017, a young girl asked Alexa to get her a doll's house, and a few days later a $160 doll's house was duly delivered. This alone was bad enough, but when a San Diego news reporter repeated the girl's request as part of the program, Echo/Alexa devices all around the area, upon "hearing" the reporter's voice on a nearby television, began trying to order doll's houses as well.[2] You can appreciate the funny side of this, but there is a far more sinister aspect to it.

When the IPA can command a door lock device to open, things become rather more interesting. When the householder is away, a thief could (at least in theory) call the house telephone, and when the answerphone cuts in, simply say "Alexa, open the door," and you can imagine the rest.

In January 2017 at the Seehotel in the town of Jagerwirt in Austria, the hotel's computer systems were compromised as a result of clicking on an attachment contained in an e-mail, and guests were locked out of

---

[2]See https://www.theregister.co.uk/2017/01/07/tv_anchor_says_alexa_buy_me_a_dollhouse_and_she_does

their rooms.[3] The attackers demanded two bitcoins (about $1,800 at the time) as a ransom, which the hotelier agreed to pay. He later changed the room locks back to normal the more traditional metal key type.

In an effort to distinguish themselves from other companies, some manufacturers develop their own communication protocols that do not follow industry standards, and while this may provide them with a degree of exclusivity, it usually means that the user cannot manage his or her device in harmony with the remainder of those in the household. Naturally, when events come about that harmonization is necessary, those manufacturers are left with the problem of rewriting their software from scratch, and the users may find that their devices cannot be updated and are now virtually useless!

One of the most serious potential problems is that of any user data that is held on the IoT device itself—most manufacturers give no thought as to how the user can ensure that this is deleted when they sell or otherwise dispose of the device.

Despite their usefulness, there is a considerable way to go before IoT devices can truly be safely used in the home environment, and any organization that uses them in its offices, factories, or warehouses must be very certain of what it is placing at risk if things go wrong.

Business Continuity Cyber Threats

Threats are actions or events that result in unwanted consequences. They are usually assumed to be man-made, where an attacker displays a degree of motivation as in the case of IP theft. Some threats may never be carried out, but the organization must be aware of them and prepared to take remedial action in case they are.

While there are no hard and fast delineations of threats, I have grouped the most common ones below, and we'll take a brief look at each in turn:

- Malware
- Social engineering

---

[3]See https://www.nytimes.com/2017/01/30/world/europe/hotel-austria-bitcoin-ransom.html

- Information misuse and abuse
- Errors and failures
- Hacking, including defacement, sabotage, and Denial of Service (DoS)/ Distributed Denial of Service (DDoS) attacks
- Loss of key information, IP and financial theft

Malware

The term "malware" refers to malicious software that is used to attack an individual's or an organization's information systems. Examples of malware include worms, viruses, and Trojans—software entities that are specifically designed either to collect, damage, or delete information, or to cause harm to an information system, its operating system, or software applications. Malware is invariably concealed from the user; occasionally self-replicating, or being attached to an executable program, and if carefully tailored can quickly spread to other systems when unwittingly activated by the user.

Some types of malware go to enormous lengths to conceal their existence, and can be disguised as legitimate software or data. However, their purpose is invariably malevolent.

Rootkits, on the other hand, are often more devious still, as they may contain a variety of malware types, each designed to undertake a different task, for example changing access permissions prior to recording information and sending it to an external recipient.

Spyware generally does just that—it records keystrokes, collects useful information, and reports back to the attacker, who may then launch a targeted attack on the basis of the information received, often using one or a number of a rootkits to achieve his or her goal.

Botnet clients are an unusual form of malware, in that they comprise a collection of slave computers—bots, short for robots—that are used to execute an attack elsewhere, for example in DDoS attacks. The bots are controlled by one or more so-called bot herders which instruct the bots to undertake the attack. Botnets are also used in delivering Spam.

Finally, ransomware has become big business. Some form of malware will cause total disruption to a user's computer—normally it will encrypt parts of or the entire hard drive—and will notify the user that they cannot now use the system. It will demand payment—usually in Bitcoins—in order to provide the decryption key to unlock the encrypted information.

An excellent recent example of this is from March 2016, in which an American health care provider was attacked.[4] The attackers demanded a ransom to unlock the computers used to access patient records, resulting in systems being rendered useless, and staff having to resort to pen-and-paper records until the problem was resolved.

More recently, the WannaCry virus caused worldwide problems in May 2017 with much the same aims and impacts. This exploited vulnerabilities in a number of Microsoft Windows operating systems, and within one day of its release, had affected almost a quarter of a million computers in more than 150 countries. Most of these were running Windows 7, and which critically had not been updated with the latest available security patches.

Soon after this, another virus known as Petya struck. Again, this was ransomware, and had much the same result. However, sometime later in 2017, a virus known as NotPetya appeared, and this—although it bore a strong resemblance to Petya—was not ransomware, but was merely designed to cause chaos, which it did very successfully.

One of the organizations affected by the NotPetya virus was the worldwide distribution company TNT, owned by FedEx.[5] Its operations were seriously disrupted by the attack, and since the attackers had not designed the attack to demand a ransom for encrypting the hard disk drives of affected computers, there was no provision for obtaining a decryption key.

FedEx estimated that the attack had cost the company $300 million. The attack has since been attributed to Russia by both the UK and US cybersecurity agencies.

Social Engineering

The technique of social engineering is widely used by attackers to acquire information concerning access to systems so that their subsequent

---

[4]See https://www.tripwire.com/state-of-security/security-data-protection/ransomware-forces-hospitals-to-shut-down-network-resort-to-paper

[5]See https://www.infosecurity-magazine.com/news/fedex-notpetya-cost-us-300-million

activities are greatly simplified. There are the more traditional forms of social engineering in which an attacker will attempt to engage conversationally with a user often by telephone or e-mail; but an attacker might also disguise malware as a legitimate web link, data, or software in an e-mail by mimicking the house style, naming conventions, or language of a major corporation. For example, the attacker may e-mail a user purporting to be the latter's bank, but where an embedded link directs the user to a website that contains malware. Some examples of social engineering threats include spoofing—masquerading and impersonation of legitimate organizations; phishing—usually a targeted attempt to collect user credentials; and Spam—which floods users with unwanted e-mails in the hope that some of them will take the bait.

Attacks have already changed from the more traditional approach to those that use psychological methods to target the user, such as curiosity, urgency, and seasonal greed.

Sometimes, however, it is relatively easy to tell whether or not an e-mail or web link is a phishing attempt simply by examining the language—grammar and punctuation especially. If the message is examined by a human, the human's familiarity with the sender or sending organization, the method of greeting, and the context of the message will allow a high degree of likelihood that the phishing attack will be avoided. However, even the smartest machine-based tool may let it through.

The incidence of phishing attacks aimed at social media accounts was reported as having increased by 500 percent in the final quarter of 2016.[6] Since then it will have increased still further as the number of social media subscribers has grown.

Misuse and Abuse

While hacking attempts usually originate from outside an organization, misuse and abuse normally originate from within it. The result may be the same for either type of attempt, but in the case of misuse or abuse, the internal user has the great advantage of already being inside at least some of the organization's security systems. He or she may also have appropriate

---

[6]See https://www.infosecurity-magazine.com/news/social-media-phishing-attacks-soar

access privileges as well as the passwords to match. Therefore, the threat from an internal attacker potentially represents a significantly increased chance of success than that of an external attacker.

Misuse and abuse threats include the modification or escalation of privileges that will allow the user to gain access to information and systems to which he or she is not entitled, and which could ultimately be passed to an external attacker. The threats can also result both in application software and business information theft.

Errors and Failures

Errors and failures are everyday events. Errors are made by users and technical staff, sometimes as a result of poor awareness or skills training, and are not usually ill-intentioned. Failures are caused by something that has ceased to work in the expected way, and again are not malevolent.

Some frequent examples of error and failure threats include software failures, resulting in application or system crashes, and also where interdependencies between software applications have not worked correctly. System overloads are also a kind of software failure, but in which the software has been stressed beyond its design parameters—for example when a DDoS attack occurs. Finally, hardware failures still occur from time to time, even though modern hardware is designed to be highly reliable. Some (but not all) hardware failures can be mitigated using techniques such as redundancy and disaster recovery.

Hacking

Although hacking's origins represent the activities of electronics hobbyists and enthusiasts many years ago in order to explore how computers worked and how they could make them work better, the term is now applied to many forms of illicit behavior. Hacking nowadays invariably results in a breach of confidentiality, integrity, or availability by infiltrating systems and intercepting traffic with the express intention of stealing, changing, or deleting someone else's information. Hacking is also used to deliver DoS and DDoS attacks, designed to prevent legitimate access to systems.

Hacking in these terms is now treated as a crime, since it almost always involves access to another person's or organization's systems without their permission.

It is becoming increasingly common to read stories in the media about hackers stealing large volumes of information, for example user identifiers, passwords, and credit card details, and then selling this information on to criminal gangs, or using it themselves in fraudulent transactions.

Hackers range from lone individuals through loosely knit or organized groups to the employees of nation-states, whether directly or indirectly employed. Regardless of their objectives, motivation, shape, and size, the damage hackers can cause is enormous, and the availability of hacking tools on the Internet (either free or at very low cost) has drastically reduced the level of skill required by hackers to achieve their aims.

The Loss of Key Information and IP and Financial Theft

The theft of information or IP can have extremely serious consequences for any organization, whether this causes customers to lose faith in its ability to protect their sensitive (often personal) data, damages the organization's value on the national or international stock exchanges, or provides its competitors with information that they can use to their advantage.

Financial theft will always remain a major threat. The bank robber Willie Sutton (no relation, I am happy to say) was quoted as saying that he robbed banks "Because that's where the money is." While this remains true, it is significantly less risky and usually more lucrative for a thief to use a computer to steal money remotely than it is to hold up the bank's staff with a shotgun.

As threats go, the theft of business-critical information or money is one that will often bring an organization to its knees very rapidly, and from which it may struggle to recover.

As we shall see in Chapter 7, there are methods that can be used to protect the business against many of these vulnerabilities and threats or at least to reduce their effectiveness.

Threat and Vulnerability Assessments

Some business continuity practitioners argue that the threat and vulnerability assessments should be undertaken in advance of the impact assessments; others will disagree and opt for the reverse arrangement. In practice, either approach will work, provided that the information assets have been identified, but it may even be helpful if possible to undertake the threat and vulnerability assessments at the same time as the impact assessment work, since the owners of the information assets may already be aware of potential threats and vulnerabilities, ensuring that nothing is overlooked.

In such cases, additional, more detailed threat and vulnerability assessments can be undertaken later in the process by cybersecurity specialists.

For each threat the assessment identifies, there may be additional data on the frequency of events when the threat has been known to have been successfully used.

Finally, it must be borne in mind that threats can cause an impact only if the information asset presents some form of vulnerability that the particular threat is able to exploit.

Summary

In this chapter, we have examined the kinds of vulnerabilities that can lead to successful cyberattacks and the various types of threat that can cause them. In the next chapter, we shall examine the various high-level options for either preventing cyberattacks where this is possible, or for responding to them when they occur if it is not.

CHAPTER 6

Selecting Strategic, Tactical, and Operational Solutions

Once organizations have a clear understanding of their information assets and the value they represent to the business, the various vulnerabilities that assets exhibit, and the threats they are facing, they will be better placed to begin development of an overall cyberattack prevention and response strategy which will form the basis of more detailed action plans.

This chapter will deal with these two principal areas:

Prevention—the proactive side of cybersecurity and business continuity, which aims to reduce the likelihood of a successful cyberattack by putting measures in place that either stop such an attack or at least reduce its impact.

Response—the reactive side of cybersecurity and business continuity, which aims to equip the organization for reacting quickly to a cyberattack that is not stopped by preventive measures, but again limits its impact.

The response strategy will also determine the approach that the organization takes to returning its operations to a normal or near-normal level.

Equally importantly, the response strategy will also deal with how the organization should communicate with its customers, stakeholders, the media, and where necessary, government or public sector authorities and regulators.

In Chapter 7, we will describe how organizations should implement these proactive and reactive measures and turn the response strategies into contingency plans to be used when required.

Strategic Options

In Chapter 2, we looked very briefly at the strategic choices for how to deal with cybersecurity incidents, so let's now take a more detailed look. The overall process of selection of the strategic options is shown in Figure 6.1.

Firstly, we must decide whether or not we can *avoid or terminate* the risk. For example, if the organization was going through the process of transferring its confidential customer information to a cloud service provider and it had been identified that this action would locate the information in a jurisdiction that did not meet data protection legislation, the recommendation would be to cancel the transfer, which would constitute avoidance or termination of the risk.

However, it must be borne in mind that this might raise two secondary impacts. Firstly, there might already have been some expenditure for work already carried out, possibly also incurring contractual penalties; and secondly, the organization would still have to find a replacement cloud service supplier if it wished to continue to outsource the information, and again this would incur further cost.

If the risk cannot be avoided or terminated, the next option would be to *share* or *transfer* the risk. This normally requires the involvement of a third party that would take responsibility for managing the risk either in total or in part, and while this might appear to be a simple solution, it may not be possible to transfer or share the entire amount of the risk, or it may be prudent to share the risk among a number of third parties.

An example of risk sharing or transfer would be when an organization takes out insurance against the losses incurred if its information is lost or damaged. An insurance company might be willing to accept all or part of the risk, but the organization would have to balance the cost of premiums against the potential losses that might be incurred if the information was lost, stolen, or destroyed.

To ensure that the cost of such insurance premiums does not become excessive, the insurer might insist on guarantees such as the provision of disaster recovery systems, and might set an upper limit on the payout, in which case the organization would have to accept some residual risk.

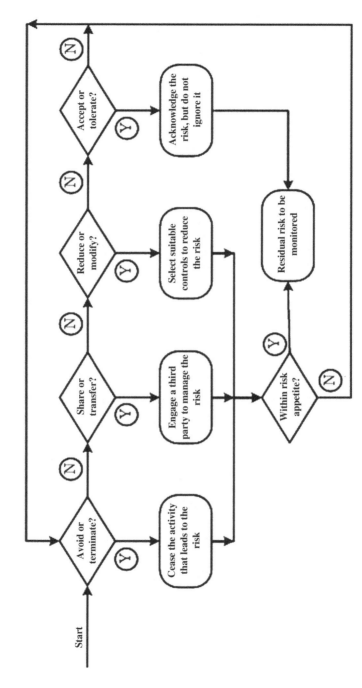

Figure 6.1 The strategic risk management process

Alternatively, an organization that placed its business-critical information with a cloud service provider would reasonably expect the provider to cover at least a large proportion if not the whole of the risk.

In both examples, it must be remembered that overall ownership of the risk must always be retained by the organization itself.

In cases where risk sharing or transfer is not a viable option, the next choice would be to investigate *risk reduction or modification*, which is sometimes referred to as risk treatment. When the organization considers the option to reduce or modify risk, it involves either reducing the impact or reducing the likelihood and occasionally a mixture of both, since there are many approaches that can be used in combination to reduce the level of risk down to a level below that of the organization's risk appetite.

An example of risk reduction would be the reduction of the likelihood of unauthorized access by improving basic user ID and password checks with the addition of a second authentication factor using a security token. This would significantly strengthen the process reducing the likelihood of unauthorized access, but the organization would need to balance this against the costs of token deployment and support, together with the additional risks brought about by lost or stolen tokens.

A second example of risk reduction would be in reducing the impact of the loss or theft of a laptop by encrypting its entire hard disk drive. Although the capital value of the laptop could still be lost (although this might be recoverable through insurance), the information contained on the laptop would be totally secure as decryption without the master password at this level is considered to be virtually impossible. Naturally, the information itself would need to have been previously backed up.

As with the option to share or transfer, the organization might accept some residual risk, such as the replacement cost of the laptop, and there could also be additional expenditure for configuration and restoring software and data. Residual risk must be recorded and monitored on an ongoing basis.

When no other options are open, when a risk is too costly to treat by any other means, where following other forms of risk treatment the risk level has reached a point where no further treatment is possible, or if the level of risk is very low, then the organization must *accept* or *tolerate* the risk. However, it is important to understand that this does not mean that it can be ignored.

Risks that are accepted must always be documented as such, and must be reviewed periodically in order to ensure that the level of risk has not changed in either its impact or likelihood, which would require that the choice of avoid/terminate, share/transfer, or reduce/modify is taken again.

Tactical and Operational Options

Tactical Controls

Once the choice of strategic option has been made, there will be four possible tactical approaches to treating the risk. These are *detective, preventative, directive*, or *corrective*, and will depend to some extent upon the strategic choice already taken. Sometimes these will be used individually and sometimes in conjunction with one another as we shall see later. As with strategic controls, tactical controls themselves do not actually treat the risks, but lead us to a more specific course of action determined by the operational controls. The overall picture is illustrated in Figure 6.2.

Let's now look at each of these options in greater detail.

Detective controls are those that permit the organization to be aware that an incident is taking place, but they can achieve nothing else—they are unable to alter either the likelihood or the impact of a risk, and they are normally used in conjunction with other types of tactical control that are able to do so.

If the warning suggests that some form of response should be taken as a result of this alert, then a separate (probably corrective) control must be initiated either automatically by the system that has detected the incident or by security staff monitoring the application. Intrusion detection software is an example of a detective control.

Preventative controls are used to stop an incident from occurring, and the choice of which operational control or controls are used will determine the steps taken. Preventative controls will reduce or even remove the likelihood that an incident will occur, and as a consequence will either reduce or terminate the risk.

A simple example of a preventative control is that of passwords on user accounts; without knowing both the user identifier and the associated password, access to the user account is barred.

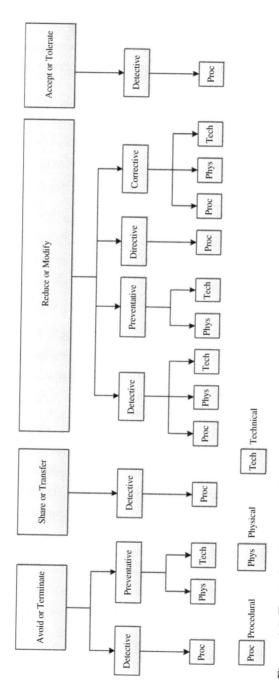

Figure 6.2 Tactical and operational options

Directive controls are normally based on policies, processes, procedures, and work instructions, all of which dictate what actions must or must not be undertaken.

As with detective controls, directive controls on their own cannot change either the impact or the likelihood of an incident taking place, since they only reinforce the organization's policies. It follows, therefore, that if staff adhere to policies, the controls will be successful, otherwise they will be ineffective. For this reason, directive controls are frequently coupled with other types such as preventative or corrective controls in order to ensure that the policies are followed.

An example of a directive control is a policy stating that users must not load unauthorized software onto their company computers. One or more detective controls might be used in conjunction with this kind of control in order to monitor compliance, and penalties may be applied for users who fail to adhere to the policy.

Corrective controls are those that will change either the impact or the likelihood of a risk, but in this case after the incident has occurred, their purpose being to fix the problem and ultimately to prevent it from recurring.

Operational Controls

There are just three types of operational control—procedural, physical, and technical.

As the name suggests, *procedural controls* simply set out actions that users and IT staff must or must not undertake in defined situations. Procedural controls alone cannot reduce or eliminate either the impact or the likelihood of a risk occurring, but are designed to do so when users adhere to them.

An example of a procedural control is the requirement for users to lock their screens when away from their computer, so that some form of user authentication must be undertaken before it can be used again. This is a directive/procedural control.

Physical controls are designed to address both physical and environmental threats, and are designed to reduce or eliminate either the impact or the likelihood aspect of the risk. They may be delivered through technical means, but the technology is normally not related to the information itself.

An example of a physical control would be an electronic entry management system that required an access card and PIN to gain entry to a computer room. This would be a preventative/physical control.

Technical controls normally refer to controls that are directly connected to the technology that supports the information infrastructure. They are implemented either in hardware, in software, and frequently in both. An example would be configuring a rule in a Firewall, and this could either be a corrective/technical control or a preventative/technical control.

Different aspects of the organization's operations will require very differing approaches in identifying the most appropriate choices for dealing with cybersecurity issues. There are no hard-and-fast rules as to how these should be applied, but in general, once the tactical options—directive, preventative, detective, and corrective—have been selected, the operational choices should be fairly obvious, but it is important to remember that more than one tactical choice and more than one operational choice may be involved in providing the final solution.

Where to Begin

It is often said that it is difficult to see the wood for the trees, and this can be especially true when trying to decide where to begin in identifying firstly the areas that might require attention, and secondly what to do about them, remembering that. As you can see from Figure 6.2, not all forms of tactical control make use of all forms of operational controls.

Tables 6.1, 6.2, and 6.3 provide an excellent starting point for all kinds of organization in understanding where to begin with this.

Critical Security Controls, Version 5.0

Table 6.1, containing 20 areas for consideration, is taken from the Council on Cyber Security's document Critical Security Controls, version 5.0[1] and is covered in greater detail in Appendix A—Information on controls. It contains a variety of detective, preventative, directive, and corrective

---

[1]See https://www.cisecurity.org/controls

Table 6.1 Critical Security Controls, version 5.0

No	Control title
1	Inventory of authorized and unauthorized devices
2	Inventory of authorized and unauthorized software
3	Secure configurations for hardware and software on mobile devices, laptops, workstations, and servers
4	Continuous vulnerability assessment and remediation
5	Malware defenses
6	Application software security
7	Wireless access control
8	Data recovery capability
9	Security skills assessment and appropriate training to fill gaps
10	Secure configurations for network devices such as firewalls, routers, and switches
11	Limitation and control of network ports, protocols, and services
12	Controlled use of administrative privileges
13	Boundary defense
14	Maintenance, monitoring, and analysis of audit logs
15	Control access based on the need to know
16	Account monitoring and control
17	Data protection
18	Incident response and management
19	Secure network engineering
20	Penetration tests and red team exercises

control areas, and will guide organizations through the most important aspects requiring attention.

ISO/IEC 27001/27002

Table 6.2 comes from the international Information Security Standards ISO/IEC 27001.

It covers 14 areas of information security, totaling 114 separate operational controls, which are described in greater detail in Appendix A. A more detailed description of the controls can also be found in ISO/IEC 27002 in its sections 5 to 18.

Again, all four areas of tactical controls—detective, preventative, directive, and corrective are covered.

Table 6.2 ISO/IEC 27001/27002 controls

Reference	Title (Number of controls)
A.5	Information security policies (2)
A.6	Organisation of information security (7)
A.7	Human resource security (6)
A.8	Asset management (10)
A.9	Access control (14)
A.10	Cryptography (2)
A.11	Physical and environmental security (15)
A.12	Operations security (14)
A.13	Communications security (7)
A.14	System acquisition, development, and maintenance (13)
A.15	Supplier relationships (5)
A.16	Information security incident management (7)
A.17	Information security aspects of business continuity management (4)
A.18	Compliance (8)

Table 6.3 NIST special publication 800-53 revision 4 controls

Identifier	Family (Number of controls)
AC	Access control (25)
AT	Awareness and Training (5)
AU	Audit and Accountability (16)
CA	Security Assessment and Authorization (9)
CM	Configuration Management (11)
CP	Contingency Planning (13)
IA	Identification and Authentication (11)
IR	Incident Response (10)
MA	Maintenance (6)
MP	Media Protection (8)
PE	Physical and Environmental Protection (20)
PL	Planning (9)
PS	Personnel Security (8)
RA	Risk Assessment (6)
SA	System and Services Acquisition (22)
SC	System and Communications Protection (44)
SI	System and Information Integrity (17)
PM	Program Management (16)

National Institute of Standards and Technology (NIST) SP 800-53 Revision 4

Table 6.3 comes from NIST Special Publication 800-53 Revision 4, and contains 256 separate operational level controls, grouped into 18 categories in its Appendix F, and also conveniently maps them against ISO/IEC 27001 controls in its Appendix H. Again, these control categories are expanded and described more fully in Appendix A.

As with the previous two examples, this list also covers detective, preventative, directive, and corrective control areas.

Incident Management Plans

The final part of this chapter deals with incident management plans. There are a number of different types of plan that can be used in the business continuity context, and these fall into one of four groups:

- Incident management plans
- Business continuity plans
- Disaster Recovery plans
- Business resumption plans

Incident management plans deal with the initial response to the disruptive incident, and will usually be completed well before the recovery time objective is reached.

Business continuity plans help the organization to begin its recovery process once the initial disruptive incident has been resolved, and may be extended, depending on the maximum tolerable period of disruption.

Disaster Recovery plans will normally be initiated soon after the incident management stage begins, as recovery of IT systems is normally a high priority.

Once business continuity plans are complete or almost complete, the plan to recover the organization's operations back to a normal or near-normal level is commenced, and this is generally referred to as a business resumption plan. In some instances, business continuity and business resumption plans may be one and the same, especially in smaller organizations.

Depending upon the organization's style, the development of plans may be centralized across the whole organization, or may be developed at a departmental level, and then brought together with others to form a coordinated approach.

An owner is required for each plan produced—preferably either someone who already has experience in writing plans of this type or someone with some level of responsibility for putting the plans into action.

The objectives and scope (both those things that are in scope and those that are out of scope) should be defined, and if necessary, aligned with other related or interdependent plans, which will involve coordination between a number of planning teams.

The responsibilities of the incident management team or teams must be clearly identified, so that everybody understands their role when the plan is put into practice.

Once assembled, the plan should be reviewed before being "signed off," following which it should be tested—initially in isolation, and once proven, in conjunction with other departmental or interdependent plans.

Format of Plans

So far, we have avoided any discussion about the format of the plans, but now is the time to consider this. As with the generic or specific contents, there may be an organization or parent company standard that must be followed.

Paper-based documentation has the advantage that no specific technology (apart from possibly a pair of spectacles) is required in order to read it, and it can easily be annotated by those using it. A major disadvantage of course is that if it is significant in size, it becomes less easy to carry around, update, and store. If versions change rapidly, as they often do in the early stages of plan development, then the waste of paper and toner can be excessive. However, some people do have a problem reading from a screen, so for them, paper may be the only choice.

Electronic versions of plans have the advantage that they can be very quickly updated and distributed, and are easily transportable on a memory stick for example. However, the media on which plans are stored must be secured against unauthorized access, and the presentation of the information must be straightforward.

Many organizations use a variety of standard "office" software applications to produce the plans—word processing software being the most common, but when it is necessary to include detailed layout diagrams, other more complex software such as computer-aided design software may be required. This can present a problem for the users of the plans, in that they would require access to all of the software applications in order just to read them. However, this can be overcome by arranging for all the documentation to be output in Adobe's Portable Document Format (pdf), which is easily readable on any hardware platform using a free-of-charge pdf reader.

Some organizations also now provide staff with briefing cards that provide them with basic information of what to do in the event of a disruptive incident.

Typically, these will include the following key components:

- A summary of the overall business continuity management structure, possibly including organization diagrams illustrating how the whole business continuity and cybersecurity functions fit together, and the key people involved;
- The alerting and invocation processes, including where reasonable, details of the thresholds at which invocation will take place;
- Assembly and rendezvous locations, so that staff who are displaced for any reason will know where to meet;
- Escalation procedures for those occasions when senior management decisions may be required, additional resources are needed, or the situation has become out of control;
- Details of alternate sites, transport arrangements to and from these, and most importantly, contact lists of key staff, suppliers, and other stakeholders.

The briefing cards may come in one of two forms—Letter, A4- or A5-sized printed and laminated documents aimed more generally at staff involved in the actual incident response, or credit card–sized folded "aides memoire" with the basic instructions for all staff, which can easily be carried in a pocket or purse at all times.

Generic Plan Contents

Plans will naturally be very specific to the organization, but will usually include a number of key elements:

Most plans begin with a brief introduction, outlining why the plan has been produced, and will describe its purpose and scope in rather more detail.

The roles and responsibilities of team members may also be described, and should some of these have variations in their reporting lines, these should also be included. For example, a team member may have the expected reporting line into his or her team leader, but may also have a requirement to report to a manager in another area of the organization.

The alerting and invocation processes should be described in detail, including the thresholds and trigger points, and again, the plan should take into account those situations in which the incident grows from a minor problem to a major one and crosses one or more thresholds along the way.

The plan should continue by describing the main activities, actions, and tasks, but may leave out the finer detail, especially if this is also contained in an operational level plan, such as a disaster recovery plan.

Any relevant background information that makes the plan more understandable should be included, as should the recovery and resumption priorities, which should have previously been agreed with senior management as a result of the earlier business impact analysis and the continuity requirements analysis, which we shall cover in greater detail in Chapter 7.

The plan must always contain contact information for key stakeholders, which might include a number of different contact options, and in the case of key suppliers, may also include reference information for out-of-hours support calls.

Finally, the plan should contain details of plan ownership and its version history, so that everybody who uses it can be certain they are working from the same version of the plan.

Incident Management Plans

Incident management plans should include the following:

- Task and action lists;
- Emergency contact details, including contact details of key individuals;

- Activities required, including those relating to people, processes, and technology;
- Information about communications, including internal communications to staff and other departments, the media, and if appropriate, emergency responders;
- Annexes, including diagrams, photographs, maps, and charts, third-party response documentation, site access information, and insurance claim procedures.

Business Continuity Plans

For business continuity plans, the information would also include the following:

- Invocation procedures;
- Locations of key people and resources;
- Procedures for disaster recovery and alternate working, including work area recovery arrangements;
- Resource requirements, including people, premises, processes and procedures, technology, information, supply chain, and stakeholders;
- Checklists, forms, and annexes relevant to the organization including situation-reporting templates.

Disaster Recovery Plans

In addition to the items in incident management plans, disaster recovery plans will include the following:

- Task and action lists;
- Emergency contact details, including details of third-party contacts;
- Details of the incident management location;
- Activities, including people, processes, and technology;
- Details of communications required, including internal and stakeholder communications;
- Invocation procedures and site access information.

Business Resumption Plans

Business resumption plans will provide details of the following:

- Ownership and management of the business resumption process, which may well be different from those involved in incident management, business continuity, and disaster recovery;
- Options for the longer-term replacement of key staff, premises, systems, services, and equipment, and where significant damage has occurred;
- Communications, both internally and externally.

Contact Information

Contact information has been mentioned in each of the above-mentioned plan types, and the list in the following paragraph gives suggestions as to the main requirements that need to be pulled together and placed in the appropriate plans:

- Members of business continuity teams, senior management, and board-level details;
- Key suppliers, outsource partners, and major customers;
- Legal and regulatory contacts, especially if the organization cannot fully maintain its legal and regulatory obligations;
- Contacts for the media;
- Insurance company details, especially if losses have been significant and the insurance company wishes to engage loss adjusters.

ICT Configuration Information

Information for ICT configurations should include the following:

- Network diagrams for all voice and data networks, both in the local and wide areas, and details of any security network equipment—firewalls, etc. that play an essential part in linking the organization together and with the outside world;

- Key computer resources that are vital to the business, which will bring a clearer understanding of what resources may have been lost when a disruptive incident occurs;
- Links to all relevant disaster recovery plans so that these can be invoked quickly, and where within the plans, the relevant ICT configuration is available.

Summary

In this chapter, we have examined the strategic, tactical, and operational options for dealing with the prevention of cybersecurity attacks, reducing their impact if they do occur, and the types of plan required when dealing with the aftermath of a disruptive incident.

The next chapter in this book will deal with the actual business continuity activities that will take place to bring all of the aforementioned into effect.

CHAPTER 7

Business Continuity Activities and Solutions

Having selected the most appropriate solutions to deal with the risks identified, it is time to put them into practice. In the past, the favored mantra has always been "Keep the bad guys out." This appears to be changing somewhat, since the new approach is one of "Detect and destroy" instead. However, it should always be remembered that while this approach may work in some environments, others such as critical infrastructure systems still require the old and trusted ways as well.

This first section of this chapter will examine how the business continuity management process operates to achieve this in general terms.

The next section will detail those activities that will be required to be in place *before* a disruptive incident occurs so that either the impact or the likelihood (or possibly both) are reduced. The final section will look at those activities that must be undertaken if and when a disruptive incident occurs, so that the organization's business can be returned to normal operations as quickly as possible.

Let us begin by looking briefly at the different kinds of incidents that can occur, and how business continuity approach can deal with them.

Failure Timescales

While the main area of focus is usually the impact of a disruptive incident, the period of time over which it takes place is also highly relevant. While we have previously talked about disruptions and incidents, we should place the terminology into perspective. Different organizations will have a differing view of the definitions, so Table 7.1 suggests one way of viewing them.

Table 7.1 Failure timescales

Timeframe	Seconds	Minutes	Hours	Days	Weeks	Months
Disruption	Glitch	Event	Incident	Crisis	Disaster	Catastrophe
Recovery	Equipment		Operations	Management	Board	Government
Method	Automatic		Process	Improvisation	Ad-hoc	Rebuild
Mode	Proactive			Reactive		

When a disruption lasts from milliseconds to seconds, it could be considered to be a *glitch*, and while this could be seen as a minor irritant, with an audible click or a flash on a screen in a voice or video call, in the case of data transfers based on the User Datagram Protocol (UDP) which does not apply error correction, but leaves this function to the higher protocol layers, the result might well be an error. However, data transfers based on the Transmission Control Protocol (TCP), which does provide error correction, should recover from the glitch automatically, although too many of these glitches would eventually degrade the transfer to unacceptable levels. Such glitches are normally self-recovering and are dealt with by the network's systems without manual intervention.

Once interruptions last between seconds and minutes occur, the disruption might be defined as an *event*, which again will frequently be fixed automatically. Data transfers based on TCP or UDP would normally be expected to time out, and voice and video calls would also fail.

For failures lasting from several minutes to several hours, the disruption might be described as an *incident*, recovery from which would normally require some form of process involving operational staff.

Glitches, events, and incidents are the kind of disruptions that organizations should anticipate and should plan to deal with proactively, making use of resilience and/or redundancy to permit operations to continue.

Disruptions lasting from several hours to several days could be called *crises*, and will generally require that the organization's line management are included in the response activities as well as IT staff. For commercial organizations, revenues would probably begin to suffer at this point, and if services were seen publicly to be unavailable, the media might well be making enquiries. For some organizations, once news has broken, their reputation could already be in jeopardy.

Beyond disruptions lasting several days, the situation might be described as a *disaster* and could extend for several weeks, which would demand board-level intervention. A disaster may severely impact numerous organizations, possibly causing damage to the Internet and Internet Service Providers, and at this level, the long-term viability of the organization could be in question, since large volumes of revenue would have been lost and the number of customers that would have migrated to other suppliers might mean that the organization would find it impossible to recover. Damage could also be caused in the organization's supply chain.

Finally, at the highest point in the scale, the disruption could be defined as a *catastrophe*, which would severely impact the wider Internet which may require the rebuilding of the whole or a large part of the underlying infrastructure, possibly with government-level intervention. Responses to crises, disasters, and catastrophes are invariably reactive, and require an ability not only to assess the situation in real time and plan accordingly, but also to be sufficiently agile to adapt the plans as and when necessary.

Business Continuity Timeline

If we now consider the sequence of a disruptive incident, the picture will be very similar to that shown in Figure 7.1.

As a reminder of the definitions of business continuity terms from Chapter 1, here is a brief review:

Maximum Tolerable Data Loss (MTDL) is the maximum loss of information that an organization can tolerate, exceeding the value of which could make operational recovery impossible or be so substantial as to put the organization's business viability at risk.

Recovery Point Objective (RPO). This is the point to which information used by an activity must be restored to enable the activity to operate on resumption, and this must always be less than the Maximum Tolerable Period of Disruption (MTPD).

Recovery Time Objective (RTO) is the period of time following a disruptive incident within which activities must be resumed or resources recovered.

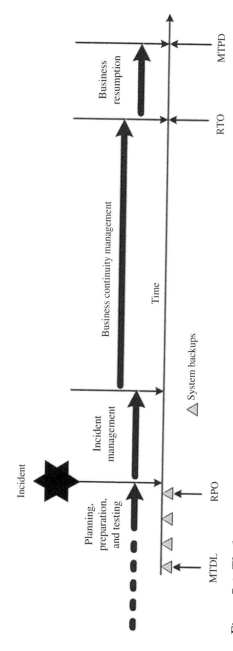

Figure 7.1 The business continuity timeline

MTPD is the time it would take for the impact arising from a disruptive incident to be deemed unacceptable.

Minimum Business Continuity Objective is defined as the minimum acceptable level for the organization to achieve its objectives during a disruptive incident.

Prior to the Disruption

Prior to the disruptive incident, the organization will (or at least should) have been making regular backups of business-critical systems, the most recent of which will represent the RPO objective, and this should at least be equal to or more recent than the time allowed by the MTDL. The organization will (or again, should) also have planned, prepared, and tested any response activities that would be required to reduce either the likelihood or the impact of the disruptive incident occurring.

Immediately Following the Incident

As soon as the disruptive incident occurs, the organization would expect to see some immediate evidence of this—perhaps the slowing-down or halting of web servers or internal systems; perhaps systems crashing or displaying unwanted or unexpected information. One would expect the organization's internal procedures to trigger a response or incident management process that would include identifying the areas affected, and if possible, applying measures to halt or reduce the impact of the incident, and also to inform more senior line management.

As discussed in Chapter 6, the organization's procedures might include incident management plans, which address the immediate aftermath of a disruptive incident; business continuity plans, which follow on from the incident management process and lead to recovery to a normal or nearly normal status; disaster recovery (DR) plans, which are designed to recover or restore the IT systems; and finally business resumption plans—the final stage of recovery from disruptive incidents, and which are designed if at all possible to take business operations back to the same state as they were prior to the incident occurring.

The business continuity management process might well continue for some time, especially if the cause of the incident was difficult to identify or if a solution was not immediately available. This often happens in cases where malware—for example viruses, Trojans, or worms—infect systems. The infection itself might be perfectly obvious, but identifying the specific form of malware could take time, and measures to neutralize or remove it would be expected to take longer still.

The organization would always aim to resolve the situation as quickly as possible, but depending upon the degree of difficulty involved, the restoration timeline could reach the RTO, after which the situation could deteriorate very quickly. If it does reach or goes beyond the MTPD, the organization might well struggle to continue in business, so it is in its interest to resume normal operations well before that point.

Planning and Preparation

It is tempting to begin this part of a business continuity management program by ticking off a few "quick wins," and although there is no reason why that shouldn't happen, it is worth remembering that what might seem like a good idea at the start suddenly becomes a bad one, and that the work might have to be undone and redone, so care is needed.

Continuity Requirements Analysis

Firstly, the organization should undertake a continuity requirements analysis. This involves reviewing the results of the business impact analysis for each product or service operated by the organization to determine what steps are required to maintain these.

The highest priority for resources will always be Information, whether it is business data or recovery plans. Next come dependencies on suppliers and outsourced organizations for the provision of vital services—IT support, power, and so on, and there may also be certain dependencies on customers who may need to invoke their own business continuity plans if the incident has a downstream effect on them. Sector regulators may be able to permit relaxation of requirements and help arrange mutual aid where possible.

External IT systems, such as credit and debit card payment systems, are almost universally contracted out to specialist providers, and increasingly, organizations are outsourcing support of internal IT systems to specialist organizations, including cloud-based application and data storage.

Firstly, for each activity, the organization must decide what would be the minimum requirement for staff, premises, systems, and information. The initial view might be that nothing less than 100 percent will suffice, and sometimes this may well be correct. However, it's worth asking the question, "Well, what if that isn't possible. What then?" Tied in with the first question is the need to know how soon the resources will be required. Again, the response might be, "Immediately," and again this might not be feasible and it is worth exploring the sequence in which resources may be required. For example, it may be that specialist systems are required and skilled staff to configure them. However, it would be pointless having the staff waiting around for the systems to be delivered, so there are the beginnings of a prioritization list appearing.

Next we need to examine the overall timescales for recovery of the activity: again there may be a need to prioritize some activities over others, so it's vital that we understand this aspect. Tied in closely with this are the requirements for minimum acceptable levels of recovery: Can we get by on 50 percent instead of 100 percent for a few days and recover something else in the meantime?

One factor that does need serious consideration is whether the situation will deteriorate as time elapses. We looked earlier at the fact that regular revenues can be lost as a financial impact, and again this may drive our prioritization of recovery.

Next, we need to think about any resources other than those mentioned earlier that are required in order to effect recovery, such as transportation, hotel accommodation for staff, and emergency funds.

Finally, we need to think about alternate methods of continuing the business functions, for example, manual workarounds, and also alternate methods of recovery, such as renting or borrowing items.

Turning now specifically to IT systems, hopefully the IT department will have a full inventory of all IT assets and also DR plans for key systems, but this is not guaranteed. Often an insignificant computer can be the vital link between two key systems and may well have been overlooked.

File, print, and e-mail servers tend to be taken for granted, but it may be possible to manage with less of these than usual in the event of an incident. Web servers also tend to be fairly high on the list of priorities, especially if the organization is heavily into online transactions, and again, DR requirements should be specified for these.

Along with the file, print, and e-mail servers, firewalls and security systems will need to be recovered ahead of other IT facilities. However, at the top of the list is the underlying network infrastructure—the cabling, wireless access points, hubs, switches, and routers that connect all the IT systems together.

Desktop and laptop computers actually feature rather lower on the list of priorities, but are still essential to the recovery plan.

Finally, we need to look back at the RPO and MTDL to ensure that we are recovering IT facilities in the correct manner.

With the increasing use of electronic mail, facsimile machines have dwindled in popularity in recent years, but still have a place in many organizations. Broadband and Internet connectivity, however, are one of the highest priority facilities that underpin communications these days, as the technology supports not only e-mail and web-based traffic, but also video conferencing and Voice over Internet Protocol technology.

Having completed the continuity requirements analysis, I would suggest that the organization should turn its attention to those policies and procedures that are necessary to underpin the organization's activities. This might sound like unnecessary work, but unless staff understand what they must or must not do in any given situation, the possibility exists that when a disruptive incident does occur, they might make the wrong decision or follow an unsuitable course of action.

Next, I would recommend that the "quick wins" mentioned earlier be adopted, but only if they are relevant to the prioritized list and they support the policies and procedures mentioned earlier.

Finally, the organization should gradually work through the remainder of the prioritized list, putting solutions into place, while ensuring that one "fix" does not impair another.

Policies and Procedures

We've already discussed the process of risk identification, evaluation, and assessment, so we'll assume for now that the prioritized list has been completed and that we're ready to tackle the policies and procedures. I'm not going to try to provide a comprehensive list of these, but I propose to highlight those that I believe will be most beneficial.

To begin with, the organization should have some basic *directive policies* for *acceptable use* by staff not only of internal systems and information, but also (when "at work") for surfing the Internet, social media, and e-mail, whether for business or personal reasons. For example, it is common practice for people with personal social media accounts to incorporate something along the lines of "My views are my own" on their profile page, so that when referring to their organization in posts, it is clear that is the individual speaking for himself or herself alone and not for the organization.

It is also common for organizations to include generic worldwide web destinations in an acceptable use policy, for example sites promoting gambling, pornography, racial or religious abuse, or any activity that might bring either the individual or the organization into disrepute. It is also normal for such policies to include details of penalties for infractions, so that staff are fully aware of their responsibilities and possible results of noncompliance.

Next, all information used within the organization should carry some form of *classification*, so that staff understand its significance and business value. Classification not only permits a descriptive assignment of the information, such as "Commercial in confidence" or "Personal," but also allows for the handling of that information to be prescribed, such as how it is stored, for how long, how it may be shared with others, how it can be transmitted or delivered, and finally how it must be destroyed when necessary. Government departments will have their own security classification schemes, and it is common practice for commercial organizations that deal with government on a regular basis to avoid using similar terms that might cause confusion.

Moving to *administrative policies*, we find a wide range of areas that may require attention.

Access control determines how systems and information are accessed by users, and an access control policy might specify the requirement for different methods of authentication, moving from basic username and password to methods such as token-based authentication, biometrics, or single sign-on.

This leads us neatly into the subject of *passwords*, the management of which is a major aspect of cybersecurity policy, and one that is not always taken as seriously as it should be.

Users are invariably lax when it comes to managing passwords and will try to use easy-to-remember passwords, such as their mother's maiden name, their first school, or the make of their car, all of which would be trivial for a dedicated attacker to discover.

Until recently, the general advice has always been to recommend a minimum password length of eight characters, incorporating a combination of upper and lower case letters, numbers, and other symbols, and sometimes to require users to change their password at predefined intervals.

In 2017, the National Institute of Standards and Technology reviewed its recommendations on passwords, and has published a new standard—SP 800 63-3, dealing with digital identity. This makes three recommendations of things that organizations should do, and four that they should avoid.

Chief among these are the following:

- The length of passwords matters greatly and longer passwords are more difficult to guess or recover than shorter ones.
- The passwords that users enter should be checked against a dictionary list of known poor or bad passwords, requiring the users to try again if the test proves positive.
- Complex rules such as a combination of upper and lower case letters, numbers, and other keyboard symbols are almost impossible for users to remember and may only result in users writing them down, which is not recommended.
- Password hints can assist users in remembering passwords, but can also provide clues to an attacker who may well have undertaken considerable research into their target.
- Credentials chosen from predefined lists are of little value as mentioned earlier.
- Forcing passwords to expire after a period of time similarly serves to complicate matters for users who should have the ability to change their password if they feel it may have been compromised.

Password policies should also stress the importance of changing default passwords, particularly those allowing root access to systems and network devices and where possible, users should have a different password for each system to which they require access.

Some application developers make a practice of embedding passwords where one application must exchange data freely with another, but because this represents a potential route of a cyberattack, it should be avoided wherever possible.

This leads into the requirement for *termination of access permissions* when employees either leave the organization or transfer to another department or role. Permissions should always be terminated rather than being modified, and reinstated at levels that are appropriate to the new role.

Unauthorized changes to systems and services are a frequent cause of headaches for organizations, and a sound *change control* policy should detail the process for making changes to system hardware, operating systems, major applications, and system utilities. This work should include functionality testing and load testing prior to the changes being implemented, and equally important is to ensure that there is a viable backout process that could be implemented if the changes should fail.

Viruses and malware can infect systems incredibly quickly, and without warning. In addition to outlining suitable antivirus applications to operate on all computer systems together with their regular updating, viruses must be attended to in a structured manner rather than in an ad hoc way. The policy should identify who should deal with the problem and the procedure that they should follow in order to identify, isolate (if possible), and remove or quarantine the virus, and how to communicate information regarding the infection to other interested parties.

Removable media is in increasingly common use, and is available with extremely large capacities—at the time of writing, 512 GB USB memory sticks and memory cards were available online at surprisingly affordable prices. These, together with DVDs and external disk drives, are all a potential route for malware to infect the organization's systems, and also a convenient and low-risk method by which users can remove the organization's information without prior authority. The policy should ensure that USB ports, memory card slots, and DVD drives are available only to authorized users, and if allowed, should always trigger an antivirus scan upon insertion of media.

In an ironic twist, in December 2015, Taiwan's national police agency handed out free memory sticks to delegates at an event that highlighted the government's cybercrime crackdown program.[1] Unfortunately at least 20 percent of them contained malware designed to collect personal data.

Shared network drives are a widely used resource in many organizations, permitting staff to transfer large volumes of information to others within the organization. However, there may not be an audit trail of who moved files onto the shared drive and who subsequently copied them. If the organization finds it necessary for users to share files, a collaborative work system (such as Microsoft SharePoint for example) might be considered, since it permits tight control by the organization as to who can make use of the system to share files, what files they can view, and retains an audit trail.

In some circumstances, organizations allocate staff to multiple roles, and this can cause serious issues if, for example, a member of staff is able to order goods or services and also to authorize their purchase, as this can leave the organization open to fraud. *Segregation of duties* is designed to ensure that staff cannot carry out multiple functions by splitting the two or more duties (with associated access permissions) into separate account types, and ensuring that no user has access to both.

A backup and restoral policy is designed to ensure that information is stored in more than one location, includes the backup intervals, the method, the media upon which backups are recorded, whether the media is retained on the organization's premises or at a third-party location (the preferred option), the maximum amount of time in which the information may be recovered, and how frequently the media is tested to verify that information can be restored reliably.

Cloud services are rapidly becoming a major force in both information storage and running online applications for many organizations who now rely heavily on this as a cost-effective component of their IT strategy. However, this approach requires extremely careful management, since it

---

[1] See https://www.welivesecurity.com/2018/01/12/taiwan-rewards-winners-malware-usb-sticks

is just as easy to delete files stored in the cloud as those on a local hard drive, and unless these too are backed up, vital information could be lost.

Also popular is the move to virtualization and Storage Area Networks (SANs). There are becoming very widely implemented, usually backed up by a second SAN which can be updated daily or at regular intervals during the working day, although backing up information to additional media is highly recommended.

Some organizations have decided not to employ *antivirus software*, as they have been alarmed by media reports that it is no longer effective, particularly when new malware is discovered for which the software author does not currently have a fix, and which are called "zero-day" vulnerabilities.

The problem with not using antivirus software is that all vulnerabilities have the potential to allow threats to take place; therefore, even if zero-day vulnerabilities occur, it is still worth running antivirus software, ensuring it is kept up-to-date and thus retaining the capability to neutralize or quarantine the offending malware.

Many of the key applications upon which organizations rely—for example browsers, "office" packages, and pdf readers—present backdoor access opportunities for attackers, taking advantage of known vulnerabilities. Their authors will ultimately produce *software updates* to remedy these, and it is absolutely essential that organizations maintain their operating systems and applications up-to-date with the most recent patches.

Automatic updating requires no further manual input from support staff, and reduces the "patch gap" to a minimum, but many organizations will prefer to test the updates in a controlled environment prior to installing them across the wider enterprise, and will also have a backout plan so that they can revert to the original version if problems are discovered.

Many organizations rely on *remote access* using virtual private networks for access both for their own staff and for third-party contractors. A policy in this area must also connect with policies covering Access Control and Passwords.

When it comes to *wireless networking and mobile devices*, organizations must consider the implementation of wireless access points around their premises; how the access points should be configured and secured, including such considerations as the method of encryption, whether to broadcast the service set identifier, and which bands and channels are most appropriate to use.

When considering devices that make use of Bluetooth for communications with the organization's network, this facility should be carefully configured for use so that the visibility of user devices is hidden and therefore cannot be detected by an attacker's Bluetooth device.

For organization-supplied mobile devices, the policy should regulate their use over nonorganization wireless networks, for example, public wireless or third-party networks.

This policy should include clear details of what information may (and may not) be stored on such devices, what applications may be loaded onto it, whether personal use is permitted, and whether or nor any personal information stored on the device becomes the intellectual property of the organization.

Some organizations are making use of *Bring Your Own Device* in an attempt to reduce the capital expenditure on laptops and other mobile devices and therefore will overlap with the policy described earlier. This policy may need to include statements regarding use of the device by friends and family, should require completely separate account access procedures, and where necessary the need to encrypt hard disks or Solid State Drives (SSDs).

Once the organization has detected that there is a *compromised system* on the network, it should be quickly isolated, so that the risk of malware being spread to other systems is significantly reduced. Once such a system has been isolated, forensic analysis should be conducted, making use of specialist organizations if necessary, before restoring the system to normal operation with verified backup media.

Outsourcing is an increasingly common way by which organizations look to save both capital expenditure and some of their ongoing operational costs. *Cloud service* offerings are key in this area, and organizations can reduce not only the equipment footprint but also the cost of initial purchase and upgrades of IT systems by contracting with a cloud supplier to undertake all that for them. The cost to the organization then becomes an ongoing operational one only, but vitally important to the contract must be some clear criteria:

- The contract must include allowance for DR of the service if either the supplier's systems or the connections between them and the organization fail for any reason.
- If the supplier subsequently constructs an index of the organization's data, the contract must make such an index the property of the organization, and not the supplier. This is important in cases where the organization subsequently wishes either to bring the service back in-house or to move the contract to another cloud service supplier.

Major Business Continuity Solutions to Cyber Issues

While some activities will be relatively minor, not only in time and effort but also in the level of change of impact or likelihood, others will be considerably more time-consuming and costly, and will have a much greater effect upon resilience.

Power is the life blood of the organization's IT systems, and the prolonged loss of it will have a devastating impact on the organization's ability to remain in business. Power resilience is best provided by combining two pieces of technology. The first is the uninterruptible power source (UPS), which consists of a system that can detect the loss of power—often by sensing slight changes in voltage or frequency—and switching automatically to a battery-backed inverter system. This is generally of limited capacity, designed to hold up power while the second system comes into operation—the standby generator which will take over the load and maintain power indefinitely subject to the ongoing availability of fuel supplies.

Organizations that are located in places where power is frequently interrupted will already have an understanding of the risks they face and will (or at least should) have this kind of facility in place. It is common practice to design systems so that more than one UPS and more than one standby generator provide the backup power, based on load sharing and with sufficient overall capacity to allow one or more units to be out of service—either for operational maintenance reasons or because of failures.

In May 2017, British Airways (BA) suffered a massive IT system failure for just this reason.[2] It was reported that an employee accidently shut down the UPS system, and that a subsequent reboot of the IT systems failed to restart properly. The consequential problems of delayed flights lasted for several days, and in all, at least 75,000 passengers were affected at a cost to BA of more than £100 million.

A similar failure—this time at Atlanta's Hartsfield-Jackson airport (the world's busiest), left passengers trapped in lightless terminals with no facilities and no flights.[3] Fortunately, the problem was resolved by the following day, but the timing—just prior to Christmas 2017—caused massive disruption to travelers both leaving and arriving there.

Physical security of key sites is vital, and it is not simply a question of putting up sufficient barriers to keep the bad guys out, but also segregating areas within premises, so that only staff who have reason to be in a sensitive area can gain access by using doors operated by some form of electronic access control and identity verification system. The ability to detect intruders is also highly recommended, and various forms of infrared and closed-circuit television systems are purpose-designed to provide this.

One of the most worrying threats is that of fire in key buildings, and organizations should always implement appropriate *fire detection and prevention* measures, so that the first instance of smoke will trigger an alert, which if verified by a second detection will trigger the release of an inert gas such as Inergen or Argonite, which will reduce the oxygen content of an area to less than that which can support fire, so extinguishing any burning material before the fire can take hold.

Cooling systems are also required to remove excess heat and to permit the IT systems to operate at a workable temperature. For resilience, it is usual to provide *at least* one extra cooling system to allow for scheduled maintenance or cooling system failures.

The organization's *networks* permit not only access to internal systems and services, but also to and from external resources. They are the means

---

[2]See www.independent.co.uk/news/business/news/british-airways-system-outage-it-worker-power-supply-switch-off-accident-flights-delayed-cancelled-a7768581.html

[3]See https://www.nytimes.com/2017/12/17/us/atlanta-airport-power-out.html

by which customers and suppliers are able to do business with the organization, and through which it and its staff are able to conduct business elsewhere. Without these, the organization cannot function, and care must be taken to ensure the following:

- The most appropriate and resilient network designs are adopted, since poor network design can result in underperformance and therefore lost business;
- The security of the internal networks is maintained, including separation between internal and external networks through the use of firewalls and other technologies.

Disaster Recovery

DR is an integral part of business continuity, and refers to the processes and procedures that provide recovery of computing systems. The main objective of DR is to return operations to normal as speedily as possible in the most cost-effective manner, but always where possible avoiding single points of failure. DR can take place at several levels, and may be provided in a variety of ways.

- Basic data or information recovery;
- Operating systems and software applications recovery;
- Recovery of the hardware platforms that run the applications and store the data;
- Recovery of premises—the offices and data centers where the IT systems are located.

All of these will benefit from some form of DR.

Data or Information Recovery

Many people would not think of backups as being a DR method, but at the level of data or information, these are its most common form. Backups are generally fairly reliable (provided that the backup media is regularly tested), but the recovery or restoral process tends to be slow, since most organizations keep their backup media in a different location from where it is normally used and where it would have to be restored.

Although the technology and capacity of data storage mechanisms is continually advancing, magnetic media still remains very cost-effective. Resilient data storage can be provided in a number of ways:

Redundant Array of Inexpensive Disks (RAID) makes use of several different methods to achieve differing levels of resilience, some of which will allow a faulty disk drive to be powered down and exchanged without any loss of data. There are around 12 different levels of RAID, and various operating systems such as Unix, Linux, MAC OS X, and Microsoft support differing RAID levels. As a general rule, RAID systems using a greater number of disk drives will always provide increased resilience over those that do not, but each method has its own advantages, disadvantages, and costs.

In *Direct Attached Storage (DAS)*, RAID arrays are connected directly to a system. Less resilient than other methods, access to DAS must always be via the system to which it is connected, and therefore represents a potential single point of failure.

Unlike DAS storage, *Network Attached Storage (NAS)* makes use of its own proprietary operating system and connects directly to an organization's network, and with the continual increase of network speeds, NAS presents an extremely efficient solution.

SANs use fiber optic links between the host systems and their highly resilient storage arrays.

Increasingly, organizations have turned to Cloud suppliers to store their data, and the capability for DR would normally be written into the service contract between the two. However, the organization should always verify how the supplier will achieve the recovery and the timescales in which they can achieve it.

Operating System and Application Recovery

Operating system and application recovery can be achieved in a number of ways. Extremely common is the use of IT systems that share the processing load, so that if one fails, the remaining system or systems will continue the processing. Clearly, a design criterion here is that the same volume of data can still be processed after one (or more) of the systems has failed. Alternatively, the organization should accept that there will be a reduced volume of processing when a failure occurs.

As with data or information, applications are now frequently run in cloud services, and likewise the organization should verify that the supplier will have the capability to provide the volume of processing when required. Some suppliers now offer to provide a predefined volume of processing under normal operating conditions, with additional processing capability brought into service when normal volumes are exceeded, and although this is not strictly a DR capability, it does provide a level of resilience to maintain the organization's operations.

Platform Disaster Recovery

This is the area most commonly regarded as being true DR, and comes in three generic kinds of facility. Some organizations operate their own DR, maintaining duplicate IT systems to provide the capability, while others choose to outsource their DR requirements to a specialist organization. Such outsourcing companies will either offer a choice of prepackaged solutions or will tailor the service very specifically to their customers' requirements. It's all a question of cost.

In some cases, the outsourcing companies will also offer office space, desks, chairs, computers, and telephones, providing a complete solution for those customers whose premises may have been badly damaged. However, these options are generally quite costly, and so may be shared on a first-come, first-served basis with several other customers.

Cold standby platforms will normally comprise a basic computer system and its associated storage. It may have its operating system loaded, but generally little if anything more. This low-cost solution requires the organization or the outsourcing company to load all the application software necessary to replicate the system it is replacing. All data must be restored from backups, and both the operating system and applications may have to be updated with any patches or software updates that have been issued. Cold standby systems inevitably take a significant amount of time and effort to bring them to full operation.

Warm standby systems normally have their operating system and all necessary applications loaded and up-to-date with patches, and may also in some situations have a certain amount of data loaded. Unless the system has been maintained in a fully operational condition, the organization will need to load any current data by restoring from the most recent backups.

While being more expensive to provide than cold standby systems, warm standby systems are invariably brought into service considerably more quickly, and if time is of the essence, present a much improved choice. Sometimes, the hardware and software of one warm standby system can be used to provide resilience for a number of similar live systems. Clearly, while system configuration may vary slightly, requiring a degree of fine-tuning when being brought into service, this approach has significant cost benefits.

Hot standby/high availability platforms are always maintained with fully patched and updated operating systems and applications. The data they hold will also be fully current, since the "active" system being replicated will be copying over all its data onto the "standby" system.

Hoy standby systems will vary considerably in type and cost, and depending upon the degree of resilience provided. This is illustrated in Figure 7.2.

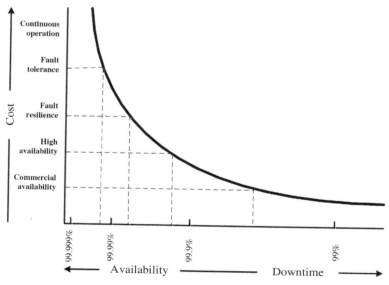

Figure 7.2 Cost versus availability

In high availability systems, data are copied between the active and the standby system in one of two ways:

> *Asynchronous replication*, in which data are transmitted from the active system to the standby system, and without receiving any confirmation from the standby, the active system continues to process data.
>
> *Synchronous replication*, in which data are transmitted from the live system to the standby system, but the live system waits for confirmation from the standby system that data have been received and written to disk before continuing to process data.

Asynchronous replication is, therefore, somewhat faster than synchronous replication, but is less reliable, since it is possible that data can be lost between being transmitted and the actual moment of switchover.

High availability systems are the most costly to provide and operate, but for organizations that deliver a service to their customers on a 24 x 7 basis, such as banks, large online retail outlets, travel companies, and media operators, service failures and the possibility of losing information cannot be allowed to occur.

Response to Disruptive Incidents

Until now, we have looked at those activities that should be carried out either to prevent a disruptive incident from occurring or to reduce its impact or the likelihood that it will occur, so reducing the risk.

It is now time to move on to what the organization should do when a disruptive incident does occur—how to deal with the incident and its immediate aftermath, and how to return to normal or near-normal operations. This is normally known as incident management, and makes use of the plans we discussed in the previous chapter.

Naturally, if a disruptive incident does occur—and all organizations will consider themselves extremely fortunate if this doesn't happen—there must be plans to deal with it. Since the exact nature of an incident is difficult to predict, many plans will be generic, and will allow for the organization to utilize a degree of flexibility when implementing them. Incident management ensures that normal service operation is restored as quickly as possible and that the business impact is minimized. It is also designed to ensure that any applicable legal and regulatory compliance requirements are maintained, and although some organizations are able to forego certain regulatory requirements in extreme situations (known as *force majeure*), these are normally restricted to those where the impact is so overwhelmingly large that the organization cannot maintain its obligations.

In the case of extremely serious disruptions, the term "crisis management" is sometimes applied. There is an excellent British Standard that provides guidance on crisis management—BS 11200:2014—Crisis management—Guidance and good practice

Turning to incident response, what we are aiming to achieve is to

- bring the disruptive incident under control, which may mean stopping something dead in its tracks, or at least slowing it down in order to minimize the impact.
- provide effective communication. This will largely be to senior management, who will decide how to present the situation to other stakeholders and the media.
- maintain the confidence of senior management, staff, customers, and the general public. The organization must demonstrate that it is in control of the situation and that it is capable of managing it.
- ensure that the business survives the disruptive incident, which is after all what business continuity is all about.

The Incident Management Process

Under pressure resulting from a disruptive incident, it is easy to lose track of the actions the organization should undertake.

The first and most important action is to understand *exactly* what has happened, especially as the incident itself may be the result of other events that might have caused additional disruption. This can be a complex process, especially when conflicting information—often reported by the media—does not provide a clear picture of the situation. Part of this process is sorting out what is fact, what is fiction, and what cannot be confirmed one way or the other.

Next, the incident management team should develop a response that is appropriate to the incident, and where there are already plans, processes, and procedures that can be readily applied, these should be used.

The organization's response will require implementation to be carried out by operation-level teams, who will report back progress, issues, and any additional impacts up to the senior management team.

Some of the early considerations for the incident management team include identifying the roles and responsibilities of the team members. Under normal circumstances, individuals will have been identified well in advance of an incident, but depending on their immediate availability, it may be necessary to make alterations to the constituency of the team—at least in the short term, until others who are better suited to the role can take their place. For this reason, it is useful to have at least one deputy for each main team member.

The invocation process and alerting of the team members should be clearly understood, and should have been regularly tested. There may be a number of possible options, so organizations should not rely on just one method, since it is important to understand that in exceptional circumstances, mobile phone networks may not provide reliable service, especially if more people than usual are trying to make or receive calls.

The team's resources should also be well understood—this can be anything from an available office with a whiteboard, fax machine, computer, and telephones to a fully equipped emergency operations center of the kind seen in news footage with plenty of desk space, computers, and maybe even a video wall to provide a wide screen picture of events.

One thing that is vital is to have off-site storage of plans and other business continuity and DR documentation in case the building that is affected is the one that normally contains all these. Consideration must be given to access for authorized staff, adequate security for the plans, a means of keeping them in step with the main copy, and above all, something that tells staff where they are located.

Finally, as the duration of the disruption is unlikely to be clear, at least in the early stages, the incident management team needs to ensure that adequate handover of duties to other staff can take place when the "shift" changes. Staff cannot and should not work extended hours under stressful conditions, and should be able to eat and rest before returning to the incident management location.

Reporting

One key activity for the incident management team will be to provide details to senior management of the nature of the incident, including areas of the organization affected and the perceived impacts, times of events, and descriptions of what is being done to rectify matters.

Information provided must be timely since out-of-date information is not useful, especially if the recipients can find out more by listening to the radio, watching television, or reading Internet news reports. It must also be accurate, and it is important to know whether any of the information received can be corroborated by reliable sources. Finally, the information must be relevant and not cluttered with anecdotal information that is perhaps interesting but not directly useful or relevant to a decision maker.

Escalation

Incident management staff must feel fully empowered to carry out their role. This includes the need to be able to escalate matters for senior management to make decisions or to make additional arrangements, when staff are or feel unable to make such decisions themselves, for example if the decision is above their pay grade or relates to an area with which they are unfamiliar.

It can also be to request additional resources in order to carry out tasks detailed within the response or recovery plan, or to notify senior management that the situation is getting out of control and requires additional levels of intervention.

However, one thing that must be clearly understood is that escalation should not be viewed as a sign of failure.

Recording Events

Incident management teams should always record events as they unfold. They need to document not only the facts about the situation, but also the decisions that have been made and the actions taken to resolve them together with the times at which these took place.

This must sometimes be done for legal reasons, but it is good practice and may be used as an audit trail for later scrutiny, and may even be used in evidence if legal proceedings follow the incident.

In order to ensure that events are successfully recorded, the team leader should appoint a scribe, whose job it is to document everything that happens. It may be possible to record lengthy conversations and conference calls, but the attendees should (by law) always be informed beforehand that recording is taking place.

Information recorded should be entered chronologically and, if on paper, should be on numbered pages to preserve the audit trail.

The scribe should record places, dates, times, events, people involved, decisions made, and the actions taken. It is also useful to note the K.I.S. principle—Keep It Simple. There is no need to elaborate—just stick to the facts. It can also be advantageous to have a second person looking over the scribe's shoulder who can check their entries and also take over when the scribe needs a break.

Management Qualities Required

Appointing someone to be the incident manager is a key task. Such a person must possess a number of qualities in order to carry out the role successfully. These include natural leadership. The situation immediately following a disruptive incident can be extremely stressful, and the incident manager must be able to pull the team together quickly and maintain the momentum. The manager should be calm under pressure, because the stress of the situation can lead people to panic and make mistakes, and a calm leader will engender a similar way of working in the team.

He or she should be familiar with the underlying subject matter—not necessarily an expert, but someone who understands the issues and can identify the right people to provide additional expertise when it is required.

He or she should be fully empowered by senior management, authorized, and where possible able to make decisions without reference to higher authority until certain preagreed thresholds are reached, or in the event of the situation worsening, when the incident manager may feel the need to seek guidance or request additional resources.

He or she should be authorized to delegate and escalate where necessary and to second suitably qualified people from other parts of the organization in order to properly manage the situation. This will also bring about the requirement for the incident manager to be tactful and diplomatic, as other managers may not be overenthusiastic about losing staff, even temporarily and in a good cause. Incident managers should, therefore, also be firm, but reasonable, and should try their best to keep other people's staff for the minimum amount of time, and to set their managers' expectations as to the likely duration.

One final point—the most appropriate incident manager may not be the most senior manager available, and this may cause friction—hence the need for tact and diplomacy, and it is also important to remember that it is more beneficial to engage with and involve staff in the work than it is to bypass them.

Communication

There are two distinct aspects to communication. The most obvious one is that of informing people within the organization and those with a close connection to it. We shall deal with that in due course, but first we should consider the other aspect which is to share technical information about the attack itself, as opposed to the impacts.

Information Sharing

Other organizations that operate in the same sector—or a closely aligned sector—can be a very useful source of information in the event of a disruptive incident. They too may have been impacted by the problem, and may have useful information on how to recover from it. Otherwise, they might benefit from a "heads-up" warning, so that they can be prepared if it happens to them.

This information sharing commonly takes place among organizations in the critical infrastructure sectors such as energy, communications, healthcare, water supply, and emergency response. Taken to its next stage, it is becoming the norm for these sectors to share information regarding cyberattacks between one sector and another, since the impact of a successful attack on one sector might well result in consequential impacts in another.

This is quite a major area in its own right, and is more fully described in "The Issue of Trust and Information Sharing and the Question of Public Private Partnerships."[4]

The Organization and Closely Linked Parties

Communication is vital. Staff, customers, stakeholders, suppliers, the general public, the sector regulator, government, and the media all have expectations, and a need to know what is taking place—in some cases a legal right, and the incident manager must ensure that regular briefings are made available. These can be in a variety of forms, but a page on the organization's Intranet (if it has one) or its main website is an ideal method. The communication should be simple to understand, and should be updated at agreed times. Ideally as a minimum it should state what has happened, what the impact on the organization has been, what is being done about it, and how long the incident is likely to last.

It is important for the incident manager to know their audience. Although each type will have a slightly different interest, if possible the incident manager should try to put out the same message to everybody, so that there is no room for misunderstanding. The organization's press office or equivalent should be responsible for translating any internal briefing into soundly worded press statements. They should also brief senior managers who will be expected to provide interviews to the media, and they will need to be extremely well prepared.

There are some fundamental rules to follow when it comes to preparing public statements—especially where the media are concerned:

- If the organization is in a highly regulated sector, a key part of the briefing will be to demonstrate that the organization can maintain its regulatory compliance.

---

[4]See Sutton, D. 2013. "The Issue of Trust and Information Sharing and the Question of Public Private Partnerships," in *Critical Information Infrastructure Protection and Resilience in the ICT Sector,* eds. P. Theron and S. Bologna (Hershey, PA: IGI Global, pp. 258–276). doi:10.4018/978-1-4666-2964-6.ch013

- The statement should tell the story as fully and as truthfully as possible, so that rumors can be avoided or quashed before they become an "alternative version of the truth."
- The part of the statement dealing with the actions that the organization is taking will help demonstrate corporate responsibility.
- The lack of a solid statement will often cause the media to speculate that the organization is trying to hide something, so an early statement will help fend off any such accusations, and reduce negative media coverage.
- Finally, and probably the single most important objective of media statements, is to preserve the organization's reputation, which once tarnished will be difficult to recover.

Dealing with the Media

Media personnel invariably have their own (often political) agenda and it is almost always different to that of the organization that is experiencing the disruptive incident—they want to break a story. The incident manager and the organization's press office must be aware of this.

The media's areas of interest are principally the following:

- Are there health and safety issues? Is there danger to staff or the public at large?
- Who can be blamed for what has happened? Having someone to blame for an incident (even if they are not actually to blame) is a key driver for the media. This provides them with additional lines of enquiry to build on and to keep the story running.
- Is the organization hiding or distorting the facts? Clearly, telling the whole story might prejudice the organization's reputation, but hiding key facts that will almost certainly come out at some stage is a major mistake, and the media can smell a lie or half-truth from a considerable distance!
- What will be the financial impact on the organization? Will the company go out of business? Will staff be laid off? Will the economy suffer as a result? All these and more provide additional lines for the media to follow and keep the story running.

- Is the senior management team capable of resolving the problem? When they can't actually find anyone to blame, the media will often revert to accusations of poor or incompetent management as a backup.

It's also worthwhile understanding how the media will try to get what they refer to as "the full story." They will often try to attack on several fronts: head office, the people involved in the response and recovery, and probably most dangerous of all, industry "experts" outside the organization, who will provide their own view about the incident and possibly start rumors that have no foundation. This is another reason for getting a statement out as quickly as possible, even if it is just a holding position that can be expanded upon later.

The media may ask slightly different questions of different people in order to try and find a different story. This tactic of divide and conquer can be very productive for them, making it even more important that everybody who might be interviewed is providing a consistent story. It is also worthwhile considering the form of words used in any media statement—if there is any opportunity for it to be misunderstood, this is what will happen, and the media will be quite content to reword the press statement to reflect their view of the situation instead of the organization's.

Organizations should resist the temptation *not* to provide a media statement or to say "no comment." If you don't give the media your story, they will invent their own "version of the truth," which might be wildly different from reality. It is often said that the media won't allow a good story to be spoilt by the facts.

Finally, organizations should beware of providing statements to some media outlets and not others. As at least one international media company is reputed to say "We're never wrong for long." The downside of this of course is that they are often wrong in the early stages of an incident, which is exactly when it would be helpful for the media to have the facts right.

Some suggested approaches that organizations might wish to take include the following:

- Using preprepared statements where possible. While many of these will be generic, having something worked out ahead of an incident can save time and effort at some of the most stressful points.

- Being flexible and quick to respond. If the organization can keep the press office fully involved and informed in the incident management process, they will be much better placed to update media statements quickly as the situation progresses.
- Ensuring that board level and local management are not only authorized but also trained in how to speak to the media. This is a skill that can be learnt. Politicians know exactly how to do this, but most of the rest of us don't. Time and money invested in training spokespeople will be well spent.
- Making sure that the story is not fallacious. The truth may hurt, but lies can be deadly and will usually be found out eventually. It is far better for the organization's reputation to take a small hit at the start of an incident than a much larger one later on.
- Finally, it doesn't matter how you try and dress up bad news. There's a saying "putting lipstick on the pig," and it's important to remember that a pig wearing lipstick is still a pig.

Summary

In this chapter, we have looked at the business continuity approach to dealing with cybersecurity disruptive incidents, and specifically how the process of incident management should take place.

The next chapter will describe the process for testing and exercising these plans, so that if a disruptive incident does occur, the organization will have a high degree of confidence that the plans will work effectively.

CHAPTER 8

Testing, Exercising, and Maintaining Plans

This chapter deals with various types of tests and exercises that an organization might undertake in order to validate the effectiveness of its plans. It also covers the process of reviewing the results of tests and exercises in order to maintain and improve the plans in readiness for responding to real incidents.

Testing and Exercising Plans

Let's begin by examining the reasons why we need to test plans. An untested plan is not really a plan at all, as it lulls the organization into a false sense of security.

At first sight, the reason may appear to be obvious, but some organizations produce business continuity and disaster recovery plans and never actually test them, and their purpose is simply to demonstrate that a plan exists!

The requirement to test plans, therefore, is to verify that the business continuity and cybersecurity approaches that the organization has adopted will work in practice, and this includes testing the technical, procedural, and logistical aspects of the plans, and verifying their timeliness and fitness for purpose. Additionally, testing plans allows the organization to verify that recovery could be completed within the recovery time objective, and to judge the effectiveness of the administrative and people aspects of the plans.

The benefits to the organization of testing its plans include the ability to verify that the organization could recover from a disruptive incident, that the plans cover all the relevant business-critical activities identified in the business impact analysis stage, and that the plans will bring about restoration in a timely manner.

When testing the plans, the organization should seek to identify any weaknesses and to challenge all assumptions that were made when the plans were first drawn up.

Finally, testing the plans should demonstrate the competence of the response and recovery teams, and give them confidence that they are able to manage the situation if and when it arises.

A number of conditions surround the testing and exercising of plans:

- They must be well planned, realistic when based on a scenario, and must have been approved in advance by senior management.
- They must have very clear aims and objectives—it is insufficient to test for the sake of it or to put a tick in a box. The exercise planners must agree exactly what outcomes they expect, or there will be no way of measuring whether or not they have been successful.
- They must always fit in with the business rather than the other way around. Whenever possible, business operations should not be disrupted, but it must be acknowledged that some disruption will probably occur when a full exercise is conducted.
- Every test or exercise must be followed by a review, in which the initial aims and objectives are critically compared with the outcomes, and remedial action is taken to correct discrepancies, fill in gaps, and remove overlaps.

It's important to make a distinction between a test and an exercise:

A test of a technology activity or procedure must have either a positive or negative outcome—it must either pass or fail.

An exercise may have a less clear outcome—success or failure are less easy to measure, but the result will still be objective, as the exercise criteria must have been established as part of the aims and objectives. It is, therefore, possible that some parts of the exercise will have been successful, while others may not.

The first time an exercise is carried out, there is a high degree of likelihood that some of the aims and objectives will either only be met partially or not met at all. The plan's remedial work should address these discrepancies, so that there is continuous improvement throughout subsequent exercises.

However, it must be remembered that even if all the aims and objectives of a test or exercise are met, real-life events may not happen as planned, so a degree of flexibility will still be required when a disruptive incident occurs.

Let's now look at some different types of test and exercise. I've included five here, although there may be variations on these that you may wish to consider:

- Walk-through test
- Communications test
- Simulation
- Partial exercise
- Full exercise

The walk-through test is simply a matter of reading through the plan with a view to making sure that it makes sense, follows a logical path, and can be easily understood by those who will have to use it. A walk-through test may happen several times as the plan is revised and improved.

For a communications test, as part of the process of producing the plans, you will have put together a contact list of the key people, and possibly their deputies, who will be required to take part in the event of a disruptive incident.

This test is the point at which you discover whether the contact details are correct and if people respond to the call. It may be useful when you make contact to ask how long it might take the individual to reach the incident management location, since in a real-world event, it might be that the deputy is closer to the location than the primary contact, and you may wish to ask them to attend instead—at least until the primary contact can arrive.

In a simulation, a realistic scenario is developed, together with suitable injects, to modify the situation during the exercise, and to which the participants are required to respond and react accordingly. Simulations are also known as table-top exercises, and generally carried out without any business pressure.

A partial exercise might be somewhat intrusive, as it will necessarily involve a number of people from various areas of the organization, and will require some actions to be taken that might be disruptive to normal operations, including preparation for disaster recovery of systems, but stopping short of an actual failover.

The full exercise, which will include a failover of systems, will be significantly more disruptive, but should prove to be a complete test of the plan. Normally, this would take place at a time when it would be least intrusive to the organization's business operations.

Table 8.1 illustrates the types of plan, likely participants, and the complexity and likely frequency of the tests and exercises.

The walk-through test will verify the structure, format, and contents of the plan. The participants will be the plan author and key users. It will not be at all complex, and once finalized, should be reviewed at least annually.

The communications test will verify that the individual team members and deputies can be contacted and that their contact details are correct. The likely participants would be the business continuity manager and (if different) the incident team leader. It is low in complexity and should be carried out at least quarterly.

Simulation exercises are designed to verify that the plan will work. The likely participants will be the facilitator, business continuity manager, any observers, and other individuals as required. Complexity is medium, and the exercise should be carried out at least twice yearly.

Partial exercises demonstrate that the plan will work in practice, but will stop short of a full failover. Again, the likely participants will be a facilitator, business continuity manager, any observers, and other individuals as required. Complexity is now much higher, and this kind of exercise should be carried out at least annually.

Finally, the full exercise will demonstrate that the plan will work in practice and will include a complete failover of systems. As with the simulation and partial exercises, the likely participants will be a facilitator, business continuity manager, any observers, and other individuals as required. This kind of exercise is significantly more complex to plan and

Table 8.1 Types of test and exercise

Plan type	Process to be tested	Participants	Complexity	Frequency
Desktop walk-through	Verify structure, format, and contents of plans	Plan author and key users	Very low	Annually, or if circumstances change
Communications test	Verify that individual team members and deputies can be contacted and verify contact details	Business continuity manager and incident management team leader	Low	Quarterly
Simulation exercise	Undertake theoretical exercise to verify that the plan will work	Facilitator, business continuity manager, observers, and others as required	Medium	Half-yearly
Partial exercise	Demonstrate that the plan will work in practice, but stop short of a full failover	Facilitator, business continuity manager, observers, and others as required	High	Annually
Full exercise	Demonstrate that the plan will work in practice, and include a full failover	Facilitator, business continuity manager, observers, and others as required	Very high	Biannually

manage, and because of its disruptive nature, is likely to be carried out biannually.

So far in this chapter we have not discussed the likely budget required to undertake tests and exercises, but clearly there will be a financial impact for this kind of work. Figure 8.1 serves to illustrate this.

Desktop walk-through tests take the time of only a few people; therefore, both complexity and costs are equally very low.

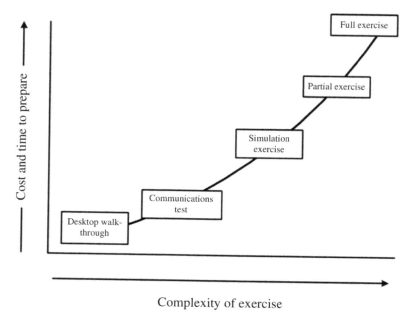

Figure 8.1 Test and exercise cost and time versus complexity

The communications test will also take very little time, but although the number of people involved will be somewhat more, the amount of time each has to take is very low and so are the costs.

When we get to simulation exercises, both the levels of cost and complexity have risen significantly, so budget may well be required and should be factored in to the overall funding requests.

The same is also true for partial exercises, when both complexity and cost have risen still further, and budget will certainly be required at this point.

Finally, the costs and complexity of the full exercise will be greater again than those of the partial exercise, and a significant budget is likely to be required in addition to board-level agreement to proceed, since it will impact the organization's operations.

In Table 8.1, we also mentioned the types of people who might be involved in tests and exercises. These include the following:

- A facilitator, who will lead the exercise. This person is probably not the incident manager, and will keep the exercise moving without becoming involved in the detail.

- Observers, who may be from other parts of the organization or from other organizations who have an interest in the exercise;
- Subject matter experts in whatever fields in which the organization is involved;
- Information and communication technology experts who will be involved for systems work;
- Corporate communications or the organization's Press Office who would play a vital role in real-life incidents;
- Information/cybersecurity staff.

The planning for tests and exercises might well follow the format illustrated in Table 8.2.

Since the costs of walk-through tests and communications tests are very low, there will be no need to agree any form of budget for these. However, it may be necessary for a simulation exercise, depending upon the scope or complexity.

The participants for the walk-through tests and communications tests should be obvious, so there is little need to have a formal agreement about them.

Likewise, scenarios and injects will not be required for either walk-through tests and communications tests, nor will a risk assessment. However, it is probably worth carrying out a risk assessment for a simulation exercise, as it may well uncover occasional issues and is good practice for the partial and full exercises.

Forward planning is essential, especially when involving staff from other departments, and senior managers and observers or participants from outside the organization, all of whom will have busy work schedules. The more notice that can be provided the better, as they will be able to plan their attendance more readily.

The timing of tests and exercises can frequently be an emotive issue. Walk-through tests, communications tests, and simulation exercises are usually best carried out during normal business hours, but because of the disruption to business operations, it may be more appropriate to hold partial and full exercises out of normal hours. The downside of this is that staff will have their nonworking hours disrupted, so again forward planning and prior agreement is essential.

Table 8.2 Test and exercise planning

	Walk-through test	Communications test	Simulation exercise	Partial exercise	Full exercise
Agree goals, objectives, and scope	✓	✓	✓	✓	✓
Agree budget	✗	✗	?	✓	✓
Agree participants	✗	✗	✓	✓	✓
Devise scenario and injects	✗	✗	✓	✓	✓
Perform risk assessment	✗	✗	✗	✓	✓
Conduct test or exercise	✓	✓	✓	✓	✓
Conduct postexercise review	✓	✓	✓	✓	✓
Carry out remedial actions	✓	✓	✓	✓	✓

Finally, it helps remind people (and as we'll discuss in the next chapter, to help embed business continuity into the organization) if the schedule of tests and exercises is published beforehand, although it might be inadvisable to publish dates and times of communications tests.

Soon after a test or exercise has been conducted, it is strongly recommended to hold a postexercise review. This need not be a face-to-face meeting, but can be carried out as a conference call. The focus of the call should be what went well, what did not go so well, and what could be improved. It's easy to say, but the call should adopt a "no blame" culture, in which those who have made mistakes and errors of judgment or who have not followed the plan have the opportunity to learn from their experience and to perform better at the next test or exercise. It is also key to identify any incorrect assumptions that were made when the plan was originally produced, to find innovative ways of solving problems and to make improvements in performance.

If the test or exercise has included the organization's audit function, it may have been a "light-touch" audit, in which observations are made and suggestions for improvement can come from the audit team. This is the best approach for early tests and exercises as it gives the team confidence that it is being supported by the audit team, rather than undergoing a more rigorous investigation, and it is worthwhile remembering that recommendations from internal auditors will weigh strongly when it comes to requesting funding for further work.

Such remedial work should be prioritized and fed back into the planning process, but should be given time constraints for completion, otherwise matters are likely to drift on without resolution. Follow-up meetings to the initial postexercise review would be a convenient way of monitoring this.

Finally, there is the question of training. Some staff will require less than others—especially those who have been involved in the earlier stages of the business continuity work. Others will benefit from one-to-one coaching, or for more subject-specific training courses, and this may also help individual members of staff in their own personal development.

Those members of staff who are completely unfamiliar with business continuity or cybersecurity and who are, or will be, involved in the incident management process will require some form of training and/or coaching before they can become full members of an incident team, and offering them the opportunity to observe exercises before taking a more active role might well be a way to provide this.

Maintenance and Review of Plans

Once we have tested and exercised our plans, we need to ensure that they are up-to-date and that they remain fit for purpose, and the program of work should include the process both to maintain the plans and to review them periodically.

It is important that all changes to the business, including business processes, activities, and acquisitions are reflected in updated plans. Any business change that impacts on the current plans must be considered—the general rule is that if it changes the business impact analysis, then the plan must also change.

Maintenance is normally carried out by recording changes as they happen when these are obvious, while reviews tend to take place when changes may have been more gradual, or after an agreed interval.

The outcomes of the maintenance and review work should include evidence of responsible and proactive governance, which shows that the organization is taking matters seriously, and not just undertaking a box ticking exercise. Furthermore, it should demonstrate that the organization has a high degree of competence in both cybersecurity and business continuity. It also demonstrates that cybersecurity risks are being considered and that remedial action is being taken, and that any changes to the organization's operational activities are being taken into account.

This visibility will be important not only to external organizations, such as key customers, suppliers, sector regulators, insurance companies, and auditors, but also to internal stakeholders including not only those staff who are involved in the cybersecurity or business continuity process, but also those who are not.

Maintenance of Plans

Let's look at some of the things we need to maintain:

Firstly, there will be the names of key individuals who need to be contacted either as members of the incident response team or who will play another role in the cybersecurity or business continuity process. It is important to verify that the individuals already listed are still those who should be contacted, as sometimes changes of staff and promotions can put the list quickly out of date. Also to be verified are their contact details, which can change from time to time.

Next, there will be photographs, maps, charts, and other documents relating to the recovery and restoration process that will change as new systems and network connections are acquired, older ones disposed of, and others are modified.

During the life of the business, third-party arrangements will change from time to time. New suppliers will be taken on, and existing supplier contracts will change, and therefore, response documentation must be updated accordingly. This is especially important in the case of outsourced contracts such as cloud services.

Next on the list for details to be updated is information regarding access to sites. Again, premises may have come and gone, and access arrangements may well have changed for those premises, and the one time we don't need access problems is during a disruptive incident when responders could require immediate access to a key building.

Insurance claim procedures will need to be verified as well, since values of insured assets may well have changed, policies updated, and the organization may even have changed to another insurer without informing the cybersecurity or business continuity teams.

Finally, the maintenance of plans should, where possible, be linked into the organization's change management process, so that those changes that go through that mechanism will automatically be captured.

Review of Plans

There are two areas to consider in reviewing plans. The first is an internal review and should be undertaken with the assistance of those staff who will take on the role of incident manager, who should be completely familiar with the plans, and who will probably also have a reasonable knowledge of business change. Next come heads of those departments for whom any specific plans have been produced. Each should be able to provide vital detail on the relevance of the plans to their department and the need for changes.

The cybersecurity or business continuity sponsor would normally require oversight of the plans toward the end of the review process, as will internal audit, who will wish to verify during subsequent tests or exercises that the changes have been made and reflect the current business situation.

The second area to consider is the external review, either as an independent audit or even as part of an ISO/IEC 27001 certification process for cybersecurity or an ISO 22301 certification process for business continuity.

The review process demonstrates competent management of the organization and the outcome should be truly effective cybersecurity or business continuity plans, and that processes and procedures are up-to-date. It will also show that the organization has an effective exercising and testing program and also an ongoing program for training and awareness (assuming that the organization has one—this is the subject of the next chapter). It demonstrates that business continuity matters are communicated to staff (especially those who are involved in the continuity and restoration process) and that links into the change management processes are in place.

Reasons why both cybersecurity and business continuity plans should be reviewed include the following:

- Business activities and processes may well have changed considerably since the last review, or since the plans were first developed.
- The acquisition or disposal of companies will have a profound effect. Indeed, if a company has been acquired, it will be important to ensure that it also has appropriate cybersecurity and business continuity plans—if they already do have them, it may be possible to align them with those of the organization.
- Technology, both hardware and software change at a phenomenal rate.
- The organization's property portfolio may well also have undergone change, and new premises will be a key element of plans.
- Staff may have changed—people leave, retire, get promoted, and occasionally major reorganizations will result in a complete overhaul of the contact lists for response and recovery, and suppliers

and third-party organizations may also have changed and require updating.

- Finally, the legal and regulatory environment may also have altered, although this tends to be a less frequent change.

Moving on to the individual components for review, the organization should be looking at mission-critical activities in order to understand whether to revisit the business impact analysis. The threats and vulnerabilities may also have changed during the plans' lifetimes, so will need attention, and this will result in the business continuity strategy being reviewed and compared with the organization's risk appetite to see what differences there are.

Lastly, there is the need to examine the cybersecurity and business continuity capability and the appropriateness of their respective solutions, together with any assumptions that were made during the earlier stages of the program, which will have determined the direction of the plans.

Finally, the organization should review the process for testing, exercising, and training to make sure that these are still valid and that they deliver the desired outcomes, and whether there is the need to perform an independent audit of cybersecurity and business continuity plans that would provide external verification.

Audit

Finally, in this chapter, we'll look at the functions of an audit, be it internal or external. Audits should not be seen as an activity where people look for problems and then allocate unnecessary hard work to resolve them. Instead, audits are a cost-effective way for achieving continuous improvement in both cybersecurity and business continuity.

An audit would be designed to verify the organization's compliance with its cybersecurity and business continuity policies and any relevant standards. There may be a temptation to change the policy to match the observations, but unless the organization has made a fundamental error in producing the policy, this should be avoided.

The audit would continue by reviewing the organization's cybersecurity and business continuity solutions against the requirements produced earlier, and would continue by validating the cybersecurity and business continuity plans against the solutions during tests and exercises.

It will verify that appropriate testing, exercising, maintenance, and review activities are taking place and that the results of these are being recorded. Finally, it will highlight any exceptions and ensure that remedial action is undertaken.

As mentioned earlier, the value of internal audit of tests and exercises cannot be overstated, since the organization's management board is likely to take audit's advice and recommendations seriously, and consequently more willing to allocate funds for remedial work.

Summary

In this chapter, we have examined the need for testing and exercising of cybersecurity and business continuity plans, and how they must be maintained and reviewed. In the final chapter of this book, we will see how the organization should make sure that both cybersecurity and business continuity awareness are embedded throughout the organization.

CHAPTER 9

Embedding Cybersecurity and Business Continuity

Unfortunately, some of any organizations' greatest risks arise from individual users of information services within the organization itself. This chapter represents the final piece in the cybersecurity and business continuity jigsaw—that of embedding their culture into the whole organization, so that it becomes a part of everybody's daily responsibility.

Additionally, we shall examine the need for skills training, in which the areas covered by cybersecurity and business continuity work require individuals who have received specific training.

General Awareness Training

One of the main benefits of embedding cybersecurity and business continuity into the organization is that it will spread the word such that the whole program of cybersecurity and business continuity work can be managed more efficiently. As staff become more aware of the need for it, they will naturally adopt a more pragmatic approach in the work they do.

It will help increase the resilience of the organization and improve its response capability, as staff will be better prepared.

Begin at the top. If the board-level executives are given even the most rudimentary training in cybersecurity, they will quickly come to appreciate its importance to the organization.

Additionally, it will instill confidence in stakeholders, including staff, suppliers, and key customers, all of whom will feel more confident in the organization's ability to survive a disruptive incident.

Finally, because it will educate and inform all levels of staff, it will help minimize both the impact and the likelihood of disruptive incidents, again resulting in a more effective response to and recovery from them.

The first step is almost always to consult with senior management to establish what they feel would be an appropriate level of awareness, both for individual departments and for the business as a whole. Their views will drive the scope of the awareness program and also its objectives.

The next step is to assess the current level of cybersecurity and business continuity awareness. In organizations where the whole program is just beginning, this is likely to be very low, but in more mature organizations there may well be some knowledge and awareness of the key issues, which should be built upon.

Once we know the desired level of awareness as seen by senior management, and we know the current level, we can carry out a basic gap analysis which will provide us with an indication of the depth to which the program must go and also the degree to which specialist training may be required.

This in turn allows us to develop and deliver an awareness campaign, which will require ongoing monitoring to ensure that it is effective and to maintain the awareness momentum.

Now we have a starting point, we can begin to identify the main audiences for this work. There will be staff throughout the organization who will, although possibly not in a frontline response role, be supporting the incident response teams, and will require a basic knowledge of cybersecurity and business continuity and what the benefits to the organization are.

Suppliers may also be part of the audience, as will any third-party organizations, such as those that support the Information and Communication Technology (ICT) infrastructure, for example outsourced organizations such as cloud service suppliers.

As with any program of work, there must be strong objectives and a clearly defined scope, to ensure that we are designing and delivering the most appropriate type of awareness training to all parts of the organization. Once defined, these must be agreed with senior management, along with any targets that must be met.

Too much information at one time can be difficult to digest, and so it may be necessary to deliver the awareness training in a number of packages, each of which deals with a different aspect of cybersecurity and/ or business continuity. The packages can then be distributed around the organization at suitable intervals.

Finally, the most appropriate method of delivery must be chosen. In fact, this is unlikely to be just one method, and there will be several different approaches, each designed to deliver a particular message to a particular audience, and there will be overlaps between these.

Moving on to the plan itself, developing the individual packages and the method of delivery might best be approached using a "storyboard" technique, similar to that used to develop screenplays for films and television programs. It doesn't have to be complicated or detailed, but if each stage is portrayed as a frame or a series of frames, just like in a newspaper cartoon strip, the complete program will be simpler to understand and to modify.

Once the content of each package has been discussed and agreed, another brief meeting with senior management is recommended, not only to ensure that the proposed program meets with their approval, but also to avoid any conflict with other campaigns that they may be planning, such as a new product or service offering announcements.

Rather than putting the campaign out across the whole organization, it might be appropriate to run a pilot campaign on a small part of the business—for example, an office separate from headquarters, which will allow the response to be tested very quickly, perhaps using a web-based survey tool, and then permitting modification of the message or the method of delivery if necessary.

The program should also include a plan to introduce cybersecurity and business continuity awareness into staff induction training, and for those organizations that make use of centralized computer-based training, cybersecurity and business continuity could well be included in the mandatory packages that staff must undertake at regular intervals.

Finally, the plan should also consider the needs of key suppliers, who may play a significant role in the organization's response to and recovery from disruptive incidents.

Now let's turn to some of the methods we can use to deliver the content. The list isn't necessarily comprehensive, but should provide some useful ideas.

Firstly, there are posters for office walls and desktop giveaways, such as coasters, key rings, memory sticks, and stress balls. Printing messages on these is not especially expensive, particularly if bought in bulk. Items that can be carried around are especially useful, as they can tend to become "objects of desire," even if relatively low in cost.

If the organization operates them, the Intranet or company newsletter is an ideal method for reaching all staff very quickly, and additionally desktop and laptop computers can be configured to display a cybersecurity or business continuity themed background or screensaver.

The agenda for team meetings is always a good place to introduce the topic, even if it is just to say "Keep your eyes open for the cybersecurity or business continuity campaign," and departments that have more expertise can run workshops on the theme. Examples of incidents that have caused grief to other similar organizations will help drive home the message.

Staff could be encouraged to look at books, periodicals, and journals on the subject, but it is probably fair to say this might work better for those staff actually involved in the process rather than for all staff, and the same applies to cybersecurity and business continuity-related websites.

A great way to make people feel engaged with the process is to encourage them either to observe a test or exercise, or for those with a deeper interest to deputize for someone in an exercise.

Finally, and most importantly, there is the need to provide structured information to all staff on what to do in the event of a disruptive incident. In some instances, this will be by a proactive message delivered beforehand, in others, it will be as a part of the incident response plan, especially in situations that are new to the organization, or are rapidly changing.

The outcome of the awareness campaign should be as follows:

- There is a heightened awareness of the need for cybersecurity and business continuity within and across the whole organization. This may take several months and should not be hurried.
- Staff across the whole organization and beyond should then have an awareness of the importance of cybersecurity and business continuity to the business, and that they should view it as an important aspect of their job.

- There should be improved effectiveness in all cybersecurity and business continuity practices, and that this should become second nature to staff, such that other business practices improve as a result.
- There should be an improved response to actual incidents—we hope they never happen, but if and when they do, all staff should be prepared and follow the guidance and advice given to them, while those involved in the actual response and recovery perform better through the support of the remainder of the organization.
- There may even be a side-effect from the program of requests for input into business development by cybersecurity and business continuity practitioners, who are able to advise on how objectives might be achieved without placing the business at risk.
- However, the security awareness training must not remain static—it must grow and develop as the threats and vulnerabilities change.

Skills Training

The awareness aspect is just one part of embedding a culture of cybersecurity and business continuity across the organization. The other is to ensure that those staff who will be required to be in the frontline in the event of a disruptive incident are fully trained in their role.

To begin with, we need to have a clear understanding of the training requirement, so first of all we must consider the following:

- What specific skills training is required
- Who requires to be trained
- What are the training aims and objectives
- Are there are any particular areas of concern
- How should the training be delivered
- What (if any) organization standards must be followed
- How the training will be funded.

Typically, skills areas will include training on general cyber issues as well as on individual supplier's technologies such as intrusion detection systems and firewalls. Also, aspects of disaster recovery, especially in high-availability solutions, will require very specific training courses. Business impact analysis and risk assessment are skills from which a number of people in the organization will benefit, as these skills are readily transferrable into other areas of the business.

Developing and implementing plans requires both a certain amount of skill and a degree of experience, as does the participation in tests and exercises, which can only really be gained by taking part, initially as an observer, and later as an active participant.

One of the most vital, and often overlooked, is communicating with the media, which should be undertaken by senior management or those likely to be confronted by the media in their response role.

Some training will be focused purely on the IT and security functions within the organization, while other training will cover all staff who are taking an active role, including those carrying out the business impact analyses and risk assessments, those involved in developing the business continuity strategy, and those developing the solutions and responding to incidents. In some organizations, departments (usually human resources) maintain a skills matrix. If such is available, it may make the job of identifying who has and has not any formal training in these areas easier.

We need to understand what the training aims and objectives are. We must know whether the organization intends to develop experts in its field, or whether it is simply seeking to bring essential staff up to a baseline level, and what the critical success factors are.

We also need to understand whether there are any particular areas of concern, such as areas where the skill requirements are high and the skills available are low. One solution to this might be to outsource the particular function, another might be to recruit additional staff who have the appropriate skills, while a third would be to identify existing suitable staff for further training.

Some people fare better in a classroom environment, while others find studying alone, online, or in small groups away from a formal environment easier to manage, especially if time constraints apply to their roles and being away from the office for a course must compete with day-to-day work. The choice of method of training delivery might incorporate both formal and informal techniques, tailored to either the individuals concerned or to the subject matter.

Next, we need to consider whether there are any company standards to be followed, such as the use of particular training organizations, remembering of course that cybersecurity and business continuity skills may not lie within an existing training supplier's portfolio.

Finally, we need to discuss how the training will be funded, by department, or centrally, perhaps from the overall cybersecurity or business continuity budget agreed at the beginning of the program.

Importantly though, there should be some way of evaluating how successful each aspect of training has been, so that a high standard can be maintained. Feedback from students is vital, and will contribute to the concept of continuous improvement.

The methods of training will include information gleaned from both cybersecurity and business continuity websites, which are an ever-useful source of good practice and novel ideas. They will often describe events as they happen, and provide background information on what went well, and what could have been done better.

Conferences and seminars are also a great way to learn about new developments in this field, including new or updated standards, meeting other practitioners, both experienced and novice, and sharing thoughts and experiences.

There may be organization-approved training courses in some of the areas we have discussed, especially in the business impact analysis and risk assessment area, as this is a very common requirement for larger organizations where risk management techniques are already in common use, and those that are in a highly regulated environment. Options exist both for classroom and computer-based training according to individual needs and preferences.

Books, periodicals, and journals are also a very helpful source of information. Some books take a very specific line, such as business continuity in the ICT environment, while others are more general in nature.

As we mentioned earlier, industry sector cybersecurity and business continuity working groups are a great way to meet other professionals, and especially those in your own area or sector.

Once the organization has an approach that appears to be successful, it may again be appropriate to run a pilot program in a key area of the business, asking the staff involved to be honest and to critique the training, and then to take the learning from that into the main program. Once the organization has developed the overall training program, it will need to assess the costs and timescales for this.

It is at this point that you may need to obtain senior management support, so you must be prepared to show that the training is relevant, cost-effective, and timely. This will lead you into agreeing the source of funding, which as we mentioned earlier might lie with individual departments or cost centers, or may come from the central cybersecurity or business continuity budget, provided that funds were set aside for this when the original program was approved.

We have spoken before about continuous improvement, and the training area is no exception to this. After any pilot schemes have run, and at regular intervals, staff should be encouraged to provide feedback on the training they have received. This will allow the organization to ensure that less adequate training is replaced with more relevant and higher-quality learning, and that new developments are taken into account.

When discussing the aims and objectives with the users, it was suggested that some critical success factors might be set. Now is the time to review these and decide what is working well and what areas may need to be improved.

Summary

This final chapter has not only discussed the benefits for embedding a culture of cybersecurity and business continuity into the organization, but also examined the need for both general cybersecurity and business continuity training, and specific training, especially in technology areas.

The remaining parts of the book are Annexes, which provide

- more detailed information on controls.
- Information on Standards—both national and international—and Good Practice Guidelines.
- a brief bibliography.
- a glossary and definitions of terms used in both cybersecurity business continuity, and disaster recovery.

APPENDIX A

Information on Cybersecurity Controls

There is much information on the controls that can be used to treat cyber-security issues. In this Appendix, I have tried to limit it to three significant sources of advice:

- Critical Security Controls Version 5.0
- International Standards Organization (ISO)/ International Electrotechnical Commission (IEC) 27001 Controls
- National Institute of Standards and Technology (NIST) Special Publication 800-53 Revision 4 Controls

Critical Security Controls Version 5.0

A number of organizations have published a list of the 20 most critical security controls. This is based upon The Council on Cyber Security Critical Security Controls Version 5.0.

While this is not a comprehensive list, it does provide a good starting point for organizations that have conducted their risk assessments but are unsure where to begin with risk treatment.

The full document may be downloaded from:

https://www.cisecurity.org/controls

The controls are summarized herewith:

Inventory of Authorized and Unauthorized Devices

Organizations should procure and run software that will scan a net-work and report on all the devices it finds connected to it. This includes

Local Area Network–connected computers, routers, switches, hubs, and wireless access points. An inventory is automatically compiled for later analysis.

Inventory of Authorized and Unauthorized Software

Organizations should procure and run software that will scan a network and report on all the operating system and application software it finds on computers connected to it. This can include both Windows PC and Mac computers, and the software will not only automatically compile an inventory for later analysis, but can also track the number of licenses held across an organization.

Secure Configurations for Hardware and Software on Mobile Devices, Laptops, Workstations, and Servers

Organizations should procure and run software that allows them to roll out a standard "build" to multiple computers, tablets, and smartphones by copying across an image of a predefined configuration rather than by installing the operating system and individual applications separately, with considerable savings in cost and time.

Continuous Vulnerability Assessment and Remediation

As with the previous three areas, organizations should procure software that will identify operating systems and application software that contains known vulnerabilities and will provide an inventory for later analysis.

Malware Defenses

Organizations should procure and run antivirus software. This comes in two forms—firstly, the "conventional" antivirus software that resides on a user's computer checks for updates and runs a system scan at regular intervals. The second type runs in multiuser systems such as e-mail servers and scans incoming and outgoing messages for malware. Both types can be configured either to delete malware or to quarantine it for later examination.

Application Software Security

Organizations should maintain continuous oversight of software applications both off-the-shelf and developed in-house to ensure that it is at the latest (tested) version, and in the case of commercial software that it is still under support from the developer. The organization should ensure that the latest security patches are implemented following successful testing.

Wireless Access Control

Organizations should procure and run software that allows them to identify all wireless access points operating not only within their premises but also within the vicinity of their premises, since users may inadvertently connect to external wireless access points that appear to belong to the organization.

Organizations should also examine the inventories collected to identify any "rogue" wireless access points that may have been introduced onto the organization's internal network without authorization.

Data Recovery Capability

Organizations should ensure that all business-critical information (including configuration information) is backed up and stored in a secure environment, and that information can be restored from backup media when required.

Organizations should also ensure that disaster recovery arrangements are in place for those systems that are deemed to be business-critical, and that the switchover facility is tested at regular intervals.

Security Skills Assessment and Appropriate Training to Fill Gaps

Organizations should identify those areas in which detailed security knowledge is required in order to protect the organization, and ensure that adequate training is provided to staff having those responsibilities.

Organizations should also ensure that all staff are provided with security awareness training on induction and at such times when circumstances dictate that it is necessary.

Secure Configurations for Network Devices Such as Firewalls, Routers, and Switches

As with the ongoing monitoring of application software, organizations should ensure that the configurations of all network devices, including switches, routers, wireless access points, and firewalls are maintained securely, and that administrative access to them is rigorously protected.

Limitation and Control of Network Ports, Protocols, and Services

Attackers will exploit unsecured ports, protocols, and services in order to attack systems, and organizations should run regular port scans, remove unnecessary services, and ensure that firewall rules are up-to-date and render systems less vulnerable.

Controlled Use of Administrative Privileges

The abuse of administrative privileges is a major threat to an organization's systems, and care should be taken to permit the use of administrative privileges only to individuals who have the specific need to use them, and to remove those privileges when they are no longer required.

Boundary Defense

Organizations should ensure that firewalls are configured to reject data originating from or destined for Internet addresses that are known to present a possible threat. Also, organizations should procure and run intrusion detection software that will identify attacks before they can cause harm.

Maintenance, Monitoring, and Analysis of Audit Logs

Organizations should monitor and record all necessary system and network activities using dedicated software so that analysis of events can be undertaken and that abnormal activity can be identified.

Control Access Based on the Need to Know

Having classified their information assets, organizations should restrict access to any of these solely to those individuals or software applications that have a genuine need to access them. Access to sensitive information can be controlled by the correct use of access permissions, or by other means such as separation of information classes by the use of Virtual Local Area Networks or by appropriate encryption methods.

Account Monitoring and Control

Organizations should ensure that user accounts are created only when necessary, and that they are deleted once expiry criteria have been reached. Dormant and locked-out accounts should be reviewed at regular intervals.

Organizations should set and maintain a password update scheme in conjunction with predefined password criteria.

Data Protection

Having classified their information assets, organizations should ensure that sensitive information is adequately protected by the use of hard drive and/or file encryption, and that any information located in cloud-based environments is similarly protected.

Further, for personal data, organizations should ensure that the recording, handling, storage, and disposal of this information complies with national data protection legislation

Incident Response and Management

Organizations should develop and test incident management processes to ensure that when harmful incidents do occur, they have the capability to respond quickly and effectively. The incident management process should include containment of, response to, and recovery from the incident, and should include appropriate business continuity arrangements.

Secure Network Engineering

The design of an organization's networks should ensure that sensitive information is appropriately protected by the use of De-Militarized Zone (DMZ) systems and firewalls and network separation, allowing bona fide users access to their resources, while denying access to unauthorized entities and attackers.

Penetration Tests and "red team" Exercises

Organizations should arrange for regular penetration testing to be carried out to verify that their security arrangements are fit for purpose. Penetration testing is generally conducted on a nonintrusive basis and is designed simply to ensure that security mechanisms are functioning correctly. Additionally, they should consider the use of "red teams" who take a more intrusive and adversarial approach and take advantage of vulnerabilities to attack systems although in a nondestructive manner.

ISO/IEC 27001 Controls

Although the primary ISO Standard for information risk management is ISO/IEC 27005, it contains no detailed information on suitable tactical or operational controls for risk treatment, restricting itself instead to the strategic level only. Instead, ISO/IEC 27001 provides an Annex containing a comprehensive list of 114 separate operational level controls, grouped into 14 categories.

A more detailed description of these can be found in ISO/IEC 27002 in its sections 5 to 18.

ISO/IEC 27001, 27002 and 27005 may be purchased from the ANSI Webstore at https://webstore.ansi.org (payment in US Dollars), from the ISO Store https://www.iso.org/store.html (payment in Swiss Francs), and from the BSI Online Shop at: http://shop.bsigroup.com (payment in Sterling).

The categories and their associated controls are summarized herewith:

A.5 Information Security Policies (2 Controls)

The information security policy controls specify that organizations should define, approve, and communicate information security policies to all stakeholders both within and outside the organization. They also state the need to review these policies at intervals, or if anything changes that might impact on the policies.

A.6 Organization of Information Security (7 Controls)

Policies for information security	Review of the policies for information security

This area of controls introduces the need for defined responsibilities within the organization, along with the segregation of duties in order to prevent misuse and abuse. Interestingly, this area introduces the concept that information security should be considered in all organizational projects, regardless of whether or not they are related to information security.

Additionally, this area deals with the need to address the security of mobile devices and teleworking options.

Information security roles and responsibilities	Segregation of duties
Contact with authorities	Contact with special interest groups
Information security in project management	Mobile device policy
Teleworking	

A.7 Human Resource Security (6 Controls)

This area deals with three distinct topics. Firstly, those controls required prior to employment, including background checks and the employment terms and conditions that relate to information security. Secondly, those controls that apply during a period of employment, including the requirement to adhere to the organization's information security policies, the need for security awareness training, and the disciplinary procedures. Finally, those controls that apply to the employee's change of responsibilities or when they leave the organization.

Screening	Terms and conditions of employment
Management responsibilities	Information security awareness, education and training
Disciplinary process	Termination or change of employment responsibilities

A.8 Asset Management (10 Controls)

Asset management controls are concerned with the identification of the organization's information assets, allocation of ownership of them, their information classification, labeling and handling, and their acceptable use and return when employees leave the organization.

Additionally, this area specifies controls concerned with the management, transfer, and disposal of media such as memory sticks and DVDs.

Inventory of assets	Ownership of assets
Acceptable use of assets	Return of assets
Classification of information	Labeling of information
Handling of assets	Management of removable media
Disposal of media	Physical media transfer

A.9 Access Control (14 Controls)

One of the larger topic areas, access controls require a policy that provides for access to network resources to which users have been authorized, the registration and deregistration and access provisioning processes. It goes on to cover the ongoing management of user access rights and their revocation or modification.

Additionally, access control covers the access to systems and application functions, password management, and the access to privileged system utility software and source code.

Access control policy	Access to networks and network services
User registration and deregistration	User access provisioning
Management of privileged access rights	Management of secret authentication information of users
Review of user access rights	Removal or adjustment of access rights
Use of secret authentication information	Information access restriction
Secure logon procedures	Password management system
Use of privileged utility programs	Access control to program source code

A.10 Cryptography (2 Controls)

Cryptography controls include the provision of a cryptographic policy and the process for cryptographic key management.

Policy on the use of cryptographic controls	Key management

A.11 Physical and Environmental Security (15 Controls)

Physical and environmental controls begin with those for controlling the physical perimeter of premises together with controls for restricting entry to the premises and areas within it including secure areas such as computer rooms and less secure areas such as loading bays. It also includes the need to protect the premises from environmental threats and hazards.

The controls continue by considering the siting of equipment, the utilities that support it, and the processes for removing it from the premises. Finally, they cover the need for clear desks and screens.

Physical security perimeter	Physical entry controls
Securing offices, rooms and facilities	Protecting against external and environmental threats
Working in secure areas	Delivery and loading areas
Equipment siting and protection	Supporting utilities
Cabling security	Equipment maintenance
Removal of assets	Security of equipment and assets off-premises
Secure disposal or reuse of equipment	Unattended user equipment
Clear desk and clear screen policy	

A.12 Operations Security (14 Controls)

Operational security controls focus on formal operating procedures, the need for change and capacity management, and the separation of systems used for testing from those in the live environment. They go on to cover malware protection, event logging, and the need to synchronize system clocks, the management of vulnerabilities, and the requirement to restrict the installation of unauthorized software on systems.

Documented operating procedures	Change management
Capacity management	Separation of development, testing and operational environments
Controls against malware	Information backup
Event logging	Protection of log information
Administrator and operator logs	Clock synchronization
Installation of software on operational systems	Management of technical vulnerabilities
Restrictions on software installation	Information system audit controls

A.13 Communications Security (7 Controls)

Communication security controls deal with the provision of security for networks and network services, and in particular, they highlight the need to segregate networks carrying different security classifications of traffic.

They continue by describing the need to manage the transfer of information across and between organizations, and include electronic communications such as e-mail and social networking, and the requirement for nondisclosure agreements.

Network controls	Security of network services
Segregation in networks	Information transfer policies and procedures
Agreements on information transfer	Electronic messaging
Confidentiality or nondisclosure agreements	

A.14 System Acquisition, Development, and Maintenance (13 Controls)

This area deals both with the requirement for information security specifications to be included in the procurement process and how application services and their transactions passing over public networks require protection.

It continues by examining the need for development rules and change control procedures, technical reviews, and secure design principles, whether development takes place within the organization or outside it. Finally, it covers the security and system acceptance testing to be carried out on all systems.

Information security requirements analysis and specification	Securing application services on public networks
Protecting application services transactions	Security development policy
System change control procedures	Technical review of applications after operating platform changes
Restrictions on changes to software packages	Secure system engineering principles
Secure development environment	Outsourced development
System security testing	System acceptance testing
Protection of test data	

A.15 Supplier Relationships (5 Controls)

Supplier relationships are key to many organizations' day-to-day operations, and consequently, the controls in this area relate to security policies and agreements between the organization and its suppliers. In addition, the controls include the ongoing monitoring of the service delivery and how changes are carried out.

Information security policy for supplier relationships	Addressing security within supplier agreements
Information and communication technology supply chain	Monitoring and reviewing of supplier services
Managing changes to supplier services	

A.16 Information Security Incident Management (7 Controls)

Dealing with security incidents requires its own set of controls, which include the allocation of responsibilities for the incident management team and the reporting of both incidents and weaknesses within the organization.

The controls then focus on how incidents are assessed and dealt with, how lessons are learned that can reduce future risk, and how the evidence (whether physical or electronic) of an incident should be collected, handled, and stored.

Responsibilities and procedures	Reporting information security events
Reporting information security weaknesses	Assessment of and decision on information security events
Response to information security incidents	Learning from information security incidents
Collection of evidence	

A.17 Information Security Aspects of Business Continuity Management (4 Controls)

In this section, we consider the controls required for the planning and implementation of continuity of availability of information services, which include business continuity, disaster recovery, and the redundant operation of systems.

Planning information security continuity	Implementing information security continuity
Verify, review, and evaluate information security continuity	Availability of information processing facilities

A.18 Compliance (8 Controls)

The controls for compliance deal with legal and regulatory requirements and the protection of essential records, how personally identifiable information is handled, and in cases where cryptography is used, how this is managed to ensure compliance with legislation.

Finally, the compliance section deals with independent reviews of the information security position within an organization, and how individual parts of an organization comply with its defined security policies.

Identification of applicable legislation and contractual requirements	Intellectual property rights
Protection of records	Privacy and protection of personally identifiable information
Regulation of cryptographic controls	Independent review of information security
Compliance with security policies and standards	Technical compliance review

NIST Special Publication 800-53 Revision 4

Although the primary NIST publication on information risk management is Special Publication 800-30, it contains no detailed information on risk treatment or the selection of controls.

However, NIST Special Publication 800-53 Revision 4 lists 256 separate operational level controls, grouped into 18 categories in its Appendix F, and also maps them against ISO/IEC 27001 controls (described earlier) in its Appendix H.

The document can be downloaded free of charge from:

http://csrc.nist.gov/publications/PubsSPs.html

The categories and their associated controls are summarized herewith:

AC Access Control (25 Controls)

Access control policy and procedures	Account management
Access enforcement	Information flow enforcement
Separation of duties	Least privilege
Unsuccessful logon attempts	System use notification
Previous logon (access) notification	Concurrent session control
Session lock	Session termination
Supervision and review—access control	Permitted actions without identification or authentication
Automated marking	Security attributes
Remote access	Wireless access
Access control for mobile devices	Use of external information systems
Information sharing	Publicly accessible content
Data mining protection	Access control decisions
Reference monitor	

AT Awareness and Training (5 Controls)

Security awareness and training policy and procedures	Security awareness training
Role-based security training	Security training records
Contacts with security groups and associations	

AU Audit and Accountability (16 Controls)

Audit and accountability policy and procedures	Audit events
Content of audit records	Audit storage capacity
Response to audit processing failures	Audit review, analysis and reporting
Audit reduction and report generation	Time stamps
Protection of audit information	Nonrepudiation
Audit record retention	Audit generation
Monitoring for information disclosure	Session audit
Alternate audit capability	Cross-organizational auditing

CA Security Assessment and Authorization (9 Controls)

Security assessment and authorization policy and procedures	Security assessments
System interconnections	Security certification
Plan of action and milestones	Security authorization
Continuous monitoring	Penetration testing
Internal system connections	

CM Configuration Management (11 Controls)

Configuration management policy and procedures	Baseline configuration
Configuration change control	Security impact analysis
Access restrictions for change	Configuration settings
Least functionality	Information system component inventory
Configuration management plan	Software usage restrictions
User-installed software	

CP Contingency Planning (13 Controls)

Contingency planning policy and procedures	Contingency plan
Contingency training	Contingency plan testing
Contingency plan update	Alternate storage site
Alternate processing site	Telecommunication services
Information system backup	Information system recovery and reconstitution
Alternate communications protocols	Safe mode
Alternate security mechanisms	

IA Identification and Authentication (11 Controls)

Identification and authentication policy and procedures	Identification and authentication (organizational users)
Device identification and authentication	Identifier management
Authenticator management	Authenticator feedback
Cryptographic module authentication	Identification and authentication (nonorganizational users)
Service identification and authentication	Adaptive identification and authentication
Reauthentication	

IR Incident Response (10 Controls)

Incident response policy and procedures	Incident response training
Incident response testing	Incident handling
Incident monitoring	Incident reporting
Incident response assistance	Incident response plan
Information spillage response	Integrated information security analysis team

MA Maintenance (6 Controls)

System maintenance policy and procedures	Controlled maintenance
Maintenance tools	Nonlocal maintenance
Maintenance personnel	Timely maintenance

MP Media Protection (8 Controls)

Media protection policy and procedures	Media access
Media marking	Media storage
Media transport	Media sanitization
Media use	Media downgrading

PE Physical and Environmental Protection (20 Controls)

Physical and environmental policy and procedures	Physical access authorizations
Physical access control	Access control for transmission medium
Access control for output devices	Monitoring physical access
Visitor control	Visitor access records
Power equipment and cabling	Emergency shutoff
Emergency power	Emergency lighting
Fire protection	Temperature and humidity controls
Water damage protection	Delivery and removal
Alternate work site	Location of information system components
Information leakage	Asset monitoring and tracking

PL Planning (9 Controls)

Security planning policy and procedures	System security plan
System security plan update	Rules of behavior
Privacy impact assessment	Security-related activity planning
Security concept of operations	Information security architecture
Central management	

PS Personnel Security (8 Controls)

Personnel security policy and procedures	Position risk detection
Personnel screening	Personnel termination
Personnel transfer	Access agreements
Third-party personnel security	Personnel sanctions

RA Risk Assessment (6 Controls)

Risk assessment policy and procedures	Security categorization
Risk assessment	Risk assessment update
Vulnerability scanning	Technical surveillance countermeasures survey

SA System and Services Acquisition (22 Controls)

Systems and services acquisition policy and procedures	Allocation of resources
System development life cycle	Acquisition process
Information system documentation	Software usage restrictions
User-installed software	Security engineering principles
External information system services	Developer configuration management
Developer security testing and evaluation	Supply chain protection
Trustworthiness	Criticality analysis
Development process, standards and tools	Developer-provided training
Developer security architecture and design	Tamper resistance and detection
Component authority	Customized development of critical components
Developer screening	Unsupported system components

SC System and Communications Protection (44 Controls)

System and communications protection policy and procedures	Application partitioning
Security function isolation	Information in shared resources
Denial of Service protection	Resource availability
Boundary protection	Transmission confidentiality and integrity
Transmission confidentiality	Network disconnect
Trusted path	Cryptographic key establishment and management
Cryptographic protection	Public access protections
Collaborative computing devices	Transmission of security attributes
Public Key Infrastructure certificates	Mobile code
Voice over Internet Protocol	Secure name/address resolution service (authoritative source)
Secure name/address resolution service (recursive or caching resolver)	Architecture and provisioning for name/address resolution service

Session authenticity	Fail in known state
Thin nodes	Honeypots
Platform-independent applications	Protection of information at rest
Heterogeneity	Concealment and misdirection
Covert channel analysis	Information systems partitioning
Transmission preparation integrity	Nonmodifiable executable programs
Honeyclients	Distributed processing and storage
Out-of-band channels	Operations security
Process isolation	Wireless link protection
Port and I/O device access	Sensor capability and data
Usage restrictions	Detonation chambers

SI System and Information Integrity (17 Controls)

System and information integrity policy and procedures	Flaw redemption
Malicious code protection	Information system monitoring
Security alerts, advisories, and directives	Security function verification
Software, firmware, and information integrity	Spam protection
Information input restrictions	Information input validation
Error handling	Information handling and retention
Predictable failure prevention	Nonpersistence
Information output filtering	Memory protection
Fail-safe procedures	

PM Program Management (16 Controls)

Information security program plan	Senior Information Security Officer
Information security resources	Plan of action and milestones process
Information system inventory	Information security measures of performance
Enterprise architecture	Critical infrastructure plan
Risk management strategy	Security authorization process
Mission/business process definition	Insider threat program
Information security workforce	Testing, training, and monitoring
Contacts with security groups and associations	Threat awareness program

APPENDIX B

Standards and Good Practice Guidelines

In this Appendix, we shall cover two areas that provide detailed information. The first area is that of Standards, which are divided into two principle types:

- Specifications are directive in nature, and tell you what should be done.
- Guidelines and recommendations are informative, and tell you how you should go about it.

In some cases, organizations can be independently assessed for compliance with requirement standards—for example ISO/IEC 27001, and the accreditation they then enjoy can be used as a benefit when tendering for business.

Standards are generally developed at a national or international level. For example, in the United States, the NIST is the body responsible; in the United Kingdom, it is the British Standards Institute (BSI); while international standards are developed by these and other standards bodies within the wider ISO. It is worth noting that NIST standards are downloadable at no cost, but many national standards and ISO standards must be purchased.

The second area is that of good practice guidelines. These tend to be developed by the organizations that are the main source of knowledge for the subject matter. While there are many commercial organizations developing good practice guidelines for cybersecurity, these often tend to be product-specific, and the wider-ranging advice generally appears at a governmental level, or from a noncommercial independent body such as the Information Security Forum (ISF), the Business Continuity Institute, or the Disaster Recovery Institute.

Other relevant standards include the American government's Federal Information Processing (FIPS) standards, the Internet Engineering Task Force, Requests For Comment, and the International Telecommunications Union standards.

ISO/IEC 27000 Series Standards

There are more than 50 information security-related standards from ISO. Not all may be immediately relevant to the reader, but I have included them for completeness. You should also be beware that the ISO standards portfolio is growing rapidly, and by the time you read this book, more may have been produced. However, I have made best efforts to ensure that the list is up-to-date at the time of writing. Where appropriate, a brief description of the standard has been included.

ISO/IEC 27000:2017—Information technology—Security techniques—Information security management systems (ISMS)—Overview and vocabulary

Apart from providing definitions of commonly used terms, this standard describes how an ISMS should work, and goes on to mention some of the standards listed herewith.

ISO/IEC   27001:2017—Information   technology—Security techniques—ISMS—Requirements

Although it covers areas beyond pure cybersecurity, this is the main standard, and it is against this that organizations can be accredited. Sections 4 to 10 describe the mandatory elements of the standard, and the abbreviated list of controls in its Annex A are described in much greater detail in ISO/IEC 27002:2017.

ISO/IEC 27002:2017—Information technology—Security techniques—Code of practice for information security controls

This standard provides detailed descriptions of the controls listed in Annex A of ISO/IEC 27001:2017.

ISO/IEC 27003:2017—Information technology—Security techniques—ISMS implementation guidance

This standard provides guidance on planning an ISMS aligned to ISO/IEC 27001.

ISO/IEC 27004:2016—Information technology—Security techniques—Information security management measurements

This standard covers the types of metric and measurements that can be applied to an ISO/IEC 27001 program.

ISO/IEC 27005:2011—Information technology—Security techniques—Information security risk management

This is the main standard used when conducting an information risk management program, and can form a major input to ISO/IEC 27001.

ISO/IEC 27006:2015—Information technology—Security techniques—Requirements for bodies providing audit and certification of ISMS

Although this standard is less relevant to individual organizations looking to attain ISO/IEC 27001 certification, it does illustrate the guidance for those bodies that provide the certification.

ISO/IEC 27007:2017—Information technology—Security techniques—Guidelines for ISMS auditing

As with the previous example, this standard is somewhat less relevant to organizations wishing to develop an ISMS program, but has been included for completeness.

ISO/IEC 27008:2011—Information technology—Security techniques—Guidelines for auditors on information security controls

This standard provides a slightly different aspect of the ISMS audit function—this time dealing with guidance on specific controls.

ISO/IEC   27009:2016—Information   technology—Security techniques—Sector-specific   application   of   ISO/IEC   27001—Requirements

This standard defines how to apply BS ISO/IEC 27001:2017 in a sector (field, application area, or market area) that has common security requirements, but where those requirements are unique to that sector.

ISO/IEC 27010:2015—ISMS—Information security management for intersector and interorganizational communications

This standard was developed with the express intention of exchanging information securely between organizations, especially when concerned with sharing information on security issues.

ISO/IEC 27011:2016—Information technology—Security techniques—Information security management guidelines for telecommunications organizations based on ISO/IEC 27002

The standard is for telecommunication organizations and will enable them to meet baseline the ISMS requirements of confidentiality, integrity, availability, and any other relevant security properties of telecommunication services.

ISO/IEC 27013:2015—Information technology—Security techniques—Guidance on the implementation of ISO/IEC 27001 and ISO/IEC 20000–1

This standard provides guidance on what organizations need to do in order to build a management system that integrates ISO/IEC 27001 and also ISO/IEC 20000, which is concerned with service management.

ISO/IEC 27014:2013—Information technology—Security techniques—Governance of information security

This standard allows organizations to make decisions about information security issues in support of the strategic organizational objectives.

ISO/IEC 27015:2012—ISMS—Information security management guidelines for financial services

This standard is important for any organization planning to offer financial services covered by an ISMS. It may also be useful to consumers of such services.

ISO/IEC 27016:2014—Information technology—Security techniques—Information security management—Organizational economics

This standard will be useful when making information security investment decisions, as will those who have to prepare the business cases for information security investment.

ISO/IEC 27017:2015—Information technology—Security techniques—Code of practice for information security controls based on ISO/IEC 27002 for cloud services

This standard will be useful to organizations wishing to become providers or users of cloud services, both by identifying their responsibilities to ensure the certification of related security controls and as a checklist to ensure that potential providers of the cloud service have the necessary security policies, practices, and controls in place.

ISO/IEC 27018:2014—Information technology—Security techniques—Code of practice for protection of personally identifiable information (PII) in public clouds acting as PII processors

This standard is applicable to all types and sizes of organizations, including public and private companies, government entities, and not-for-profit organizations, which provide information processing services as PII processors via cloud computing under contract to other organizations.

ISO/IEC 27019:2017—Information technology—Security techniques—Information security management guidelines based on ISO/IEC 27002 for process control systems specific to the energy utility industry

This standard is important for any organization in the energy utility sector planning to operate an ISMS. It may also be useful to related organizations such as utility plant suppliers, systems integrators, and auditors.

BS ISO/IEC 27021:2017—Information technology. Security techniques. Competence requirements for ISMS professionals

ISO/IEC 27031:2011—Information technology—Security techniques—Guidelines for information and communication technology readiness for business continuity

This standard provides guidelines for the preparation of information and communications technology systems in meeting business continuity requirements, and relates to ISO 22301.

ISO/IEC 27032:2012—Information technology—Security techniques—Guidelines for cybersecurity

This standard will be of much greater value to those organizations that are investing in protection against cybersecurity problems. It provides a detailed framework for identifying cybersecurity issues and a high-level set of controls for dealing with them.

ISO/IEC 27033–1:2015—Information technology—Security techniques—Network security—Overview and concepts

The first of five standards relating to network security, this standard deals with the main issues that organizations are likely to face.

ISO/IEC   27033–2:2012—Information   technology—Security techniques—Guidelines for the design and implementation of network security

This standard takes matters to the next level and defines the network security requirements that are likely to be needed, and provides a checklist.

ISO/IEC   27033–3:2010—Information   technology—Security techniques—Network   security—Reference   networking   scenarios— Threats, design techniques, and control issues

This standard deals with security network design principles, and examines the threats and possible controls associated with them.

ISO/IEC   27033–4:2014—Information   technology—Security techniques—Network security—Securing communications between networks using security gateways

This standard provides guidance on securing communications between networks using security gateways and firewalls, and introduces the concept of both intrusion detection systems (IDS) and intrusion prevention systems (IPS).

ISO/IEC   27033–5:2013—Information   technology—Security techniques—Network security—Securing communications across networks using Virtual Private Networks (VPNs)

The final part of this standard deals with securing network interconnections and how to connect remote users by providing VPNs.

BS ISO/IEC 27033-6:2016—Information technology Security techniques Network security Securing wireless IP network access

ISO/IEC   27034–1:2011—Information   technology—Security techniques—Application security—Overview and concepts

This standard sets the scene for the secure development of applications, and in particular, deals with the application of security management process.

ISO/IEC 27034–2:2015 – Information technology—Security techniques—Application security—Organization normative framework

STANDARDS AND GOOD PRACTICE GUIDELINES   155

This standard follows on from ISO/IEC 27034-1, and provides more detailed guidance on the implementation of application security, including a detailed description of the application security life cycle reference model.

ISO/IEC 27035:2011—Information technology—Security techniques—Information security incident management

This standard deals with the management of cybersecurity incidents.

ISO/IEC 27034-5:2017—Information technology—Security techniques—Application security—Protocols and application security controls data structure

ISO/IEC 27034-6:2016—Information technology—Security techniques—Application security—Case studies

ISO/IEC 27035-1:2016—Information technology—Security techniques—Information security incident management—Principles of incident management

ISO/IEC 27035-2:2016—Information technology—Security techniques—Information security incident management—Guidelines to plan and prepare for incident response

ISO/IEC 27036–1:2014—Information technology—Security techniques—Information security for supplier relationships—Overview and concepts

This series of three standards examines the security requirements for the relationship between organizations and their suppliers. A fourth standard is currently under development which will cover cloud supplier relationships.

ISO/IEC 27036–2:2014—Information technology—Security techniques—Information security for supplier relationships— Requirements

This standard goes into greater detail regarding the technical security requirements that must be agreed and managed between an organization and its suppliers.

ISO/IEC 27036–3:2013—Information technology—Security techniques—Information security for supplier relationships—Guidelines for information and communication technology supply chain security

Frequently, supply chains are multilayered and global, and this third standard in the series provides guidance on managing the complex risk environment.

ISO/IEC 27037:2016—Information technology—Security techniques—Guidelines for the identification, collection, acquisition, and preservation of digital evidence

When cyber incidents occur, it may be necessary to preserve evidence of the fact, and this standard provides guidelines for the forensic preservation of evidence.

ISO/IEC 27038:2016—Information technology—Security techniques—Specification for digital redaction

When organizations require to anonymize information within a document or to redact it completely, this standard provides guidelines on the process and techniques, and may be useful in information-sharing situations.

ISO/IEC 27039:2015—Information technology—Security techniques—Selection, deployment, and operations of IDPS

IDPS can provide an analysis of host and network traffic and/or audit trails for attack signatures or specific patterns that usually indicate malicious or suspicious intent. This Standard provides guidelines for effective IDPS selection, deployment, and operation, as well as fundamental knowledge about IDPS.

ISO/IEC 27040:2016—Information technology—Security techniques—Storage security

This standard applies to all data owners, ICT managers, and security officers from small enterprises to global organizations, as well as manufacturers of general and specialized data storage products, and is particularly relevant to data destruction services.

ISO/IEC 27041:2016—Information technology—Security techniques—Guidance on assuring the suitability and adequacy of incident investigative method

This standard contains an assurance model with details of how to validate the methods used for investigations and shows how internal and external resources can be used to carry out assurance.

ISO/IEC 27042:2016—Information technology—Security techniques—Guidelines for the analysis and interpretation of digital evidence

This standard provides a detailed framework for investigation, giving guidance on how to structure and prioritize investigative stages in order to produce analysis and reports that can be used to improve security in the future.

ISO/IEC 27043:2016—Information technology. Security techniques. Incident investigation principles and processes

This standard is intended to aid in digital investigations, with the aim that a suitably skilled investigator should obtain the same result as another similarly skilled investigator, working under similar conditions.

ISO/IEC 27050-3:2017—Information technology—Security techniques—Electronic discovery—Code of practice for electronic discovery

ISO/IEC 27050-3:2017—Information technology—Security techniques—Electronic discovery—Code of practice for electronic discovery

Other Relevant ISO Standards

ISO/IEC 17788:2014—Information technology—Cloud computing—Overview and vocabulary, and

ISO/IEC 17789:2014—Information technology—Cloud computing—Reference architecture

These two standards should appeal to all kinds of cloud customers—from small enterprises to global organizations—and to all kinds of cloud providers and partner organizations such as software developers and auditors.

ISO/IEC 24762:2008—Information technology—Security techniques—Guidelines for information and communications technology disaster recovery services

This standard takes us into the area of disaster recovery, and is aimed at aiding the operation of an ISMS by providing guidance on the provision of information and communications technology disaster recovery services as part of business continuity management.

ISO/IEC 29100:2011—Information technology—Security techniques—Privacy framework

This standard provides a high-level framework for the protection of PII within ICT systems.

ISO/IEC 29101:2013—Information technology—Security techniques—Privacy architecture framework

The guidance in this standard is applicable to entities involved in specifying, procuring, architecting, designing, testing, maintaining, administering, and operating ICT systems that process PII. It focuses primarily on ICT systems that are designed to interact with PII principles.

ISO/IEC 29147:2014—Information technology—Security techniques—Vulnerability disclosure

This standard provides guidelines for vendors to be included in their business processes when receiving information about potential vulnerabilities and distributing vulnerability resolution information.

ISO/IEC 29190:2015—Information technology—Security techniques—Privacy capability assessment model

This standard provides guidance for organizations in producing an overall "score" against a simple capability assessment model; a set of metrics indicating assessment against key performance indicators; and the detailed outputs from privacy process management audits and management practices.

ISO/IEC 30111:2013—Information technology—Security techniques—Vulnerability handling processes

This standard describes processes for vendors to handle reports of potential vulnerabilities in products and online services.

Business Continuity Standards

The following is a list of the most relevant standards and good practice guidelines, and includes standards relating to incident and crisis management, both of which may be required as part of a business continuity program, and especially in response to a cybersecurity incident.

ISO 22300:2014—Societal security—Terminology

ISO 22301:2014 Societal security—Business continuity management systems—Requirements. It specifies the requirements to

- identify crucial risk factors already affecting your organization.
- understand your organization's needs and obligations.
- establish, implement, and maintain your BCMS.
- measure your organization's overall capability to manage disruptive incidents.
- guarantee conformity with stated business continuity policy.

ISO 22313:2014—Societal security—Business continuity management systems—Guidance

ISO 22316:2017—Security and resilience—Organizational resilience—Principles and attributes. It provides terminology relating to, and the principles for, organizational resilience. It identifies attributes and activities that support an organization in enhancing its organizational resilience.

PD ISO/TS 22317:2015—Societal security—Business continuity management systems—Guidelines for business impact analysis

ISO 22318:2015—Societal security—Business continuity management systems—Guidelines for supply chain continuity

ISO 22320:2011 Ed 1—Societal security—Emergency management—Requirements for incident response

ISO 22322:2015—Societal security—Emergency management—Guidelines for public warning

ISO 22325:2016—Security and resilience—Emergency management—Guidelines for capability assessment

ISO/IEC 24762:2008—Information technology. Security techniques. Guidelines for information and communications technology disaster recovery services

ISO/IEC 27031:2011 Guidelines for information and communication technology readiness for business continuity

ISO 22324:2015—Societal security—Emergency management—Guidelines for color-coded alerts

PD 25111:2010—Business continuity management—Guidance on the human aspects of business continuity

PD 25666:2010—Business continuity management. Guidance on exercising and testing for continuity and contingency programs

BS 11200:2014—Crisis management. Guidance and good practice

PAS 77:2006 IT Service Continuity Management—Code of Practice.

All the aforementioned BS and ISO standards can be purchased in either hard copy or electronic form (pdf) from the ANSI Webstore at https://webstore.ansi.org (payment in US Dollars), from the ISO Store https://www.iso.org/store.html (payment in Swiss Francs), and from the BSI Online Shop at: http://shop.bsigroup.com (payment in Sterling).

NIST Standards

At the time of writing, there are around 185 NIST SP 800 series standards relating to information security—there are rather too many to list individually here and the list is being added to all the time, and can be found at: https://csrc.nist.gov/publications/sp800

Also at the time of writing, there are 11 NIST Draft Cyber Security guides in the SP-1800 series at: https://csrc.nist.gov/publications/sp1800. Some of these are still in draft form.

SP 1800-1	Securing Electronic Health Records on Mobile Devices
SP 1800-2	Identity and Access Management for Electric Utilities
SP 1800-3	Attribute Based Access Control (2nd Draft)
SP 1800-4	Mobile Device Security: Cloud and Hybrid Builds
SP 1800-5	IT Asset Management: Financial Services
SP 1800-6	Domain Name System-Based Electronic Mail Security
SP 1800-7	Situational Awareness for Electric Utilities
SP 1800-8	Securing Wireless Infusion Pumps in Healthcare Delivery Organizations

SP 1800-9	Access Rights Management for the Financial Services Sector
SP 1800-11	Data Integrity: Recovering from Ransomware and Other Destructive Events
SP 1800-12	Derived Personal Identity Verification (PIV) Credentials

The Federal Information Processing (FIPS) Standards

These are nine relevant FIPS Standards, available at https://csrc.nist.gov/publications/fips

FIPS 140-2	Security Requirements for Cryptographic Modules
FIPS 180-4	Secure Hash Standard
FIPS 186-4	Digital Signature Standard
FIPS 197	Advanced Encryption Standard
FIPS 198-1	The Keyed-Hash Message Authentication Code
FIPS 199	Standards for Security Categorization of Federal Information and Information
FIPS 200	Minimum Security Requirements for Federal Information and Information
FIPS 201-2	PIV of Federal Employees and Contractors

Good Practice Guidelines

There are many examples of good practice guidelines on the Internet, making it an impossible task to list them all. However, the following are of particular note, and will direct the reader to those guidelines of interest and will provide the level of detail required.

NIST

Details of the NIST Framework for Improving Critical Infrastructure Cybersecurity can be found at https://www.nist.gov/cyberframework

NIST has also published a document entitles Small Business Information Security: The Fundamentals, which can be downloaded from: https://nvlpubs.nist.gov/nistpubs/ir/2016/NIST.IR.7621r1.pdf

US-CERT (United States Computer Emergency Readiness Team)

US-CERT is tasked with responding to major incidents, analyzing threats, and exchanging critical cybersecurity information with trusted partners around the world in addition to providing its users with alerts, current activity, bulletins, and tips. https://www.us-cert.gov/ncas

Information Security Forum (ISF)

Organizations that are members of the ISF have access to the Forum Standard of Good Practice, the most recent version being from 2013. See https://www.securityforum.org/tool/the-isf-standardrmation-security/

CESG

CESG (National Technical Authority for Information Assurance, formerly Communications-Electronics Security Group), the Information Security Arm of the UK's GCHQ has produced a document entitled "10 Steps to Cyber Security."

Glossary and Definitions

Acceptable use. A policy used to identify what personal use of company resources is acceptable

Accountability. The attribute of having to answer for one's actions

Accredited. Acknowledgment by an official body that an individual or entity has met predefined criteria

Active content. Active content is content on a website that is either interactive, such as Internet polls or dynamic, such as animated pictures, JavaScript applications, or ActiveX applications.

Analysis. The detailed examination of the elements or structure of an entity

Antivirus. Software designed to negate or destroy a computer virus

Assessment. An estimation of the nature or quality of an entity

Asset. Something that has a value to an organization

Assurance. A positive acknowledgment designed to provide confidence

Asymmetric cryptography. A cryptographic system requiring two separate keys, one of which is secret and one of which is public

Audit. A formal inspection of an organization's processes or procedures

Authentication. The assurance that a person or entity is who they claim to be

Authorization. An official sanction that an individual is permitted to carry out a task or to have access to information

Availability. The property of being accessible when required by an authorized person, entity, or process.

Back door. A back door is a method of bypassing normal authentication methods, securing illegal remote access to a computer.

Baseline controls. Baseline controls are standards that are used to define how systems should be configured and managed.

Biometrics. Biometric identifiers are the distinctive, measurable characteristics used to label and describe individuals.

Black hat. A term generally applied to a hacker who regularly attacks computer systems

Botnet. A network of private computers infected with malicious software and controlled as a group without the owners' knowledge

Business Continuity. The ability of an organization to continue to function in order to deliver its products or services at an acceptable level following a business disruption

Business Impact Analysis. The process of analyzing the consequences of a business disruption that might impact the organization's assets

Certification. A process confirming that a person has reached a predefined level of achievement

Classification. The arrangement of items into taxonomic groups

Code of conduct. A policy that may apply to individuals in order to ensure that they behave in a certain way

Compliance. To act in accordance with a set of rules or a policy

Confidentiality. The property that information is prevented from being available or disclosed to unauthorized persons, entities, or processes

Corrective controls. A form of risk treatment, corrective controls are applied after an event to prevent it from recurring

Countermeasure. An action taken to counteract a threat

Cover time. The minimum time for which information must remain secret

Cryptanalysis. Cryptanalysis is used to breach cryptographic security systems and gain access to the contents of encrypted messages.

Cryptography. Literally, hidden or secret writing, cryptography is the practice and study of techniques for secure communication in the presence of third parties.

Decryption. Decryption is the process of taking encrypted information and returning it to a state of plain text.

Denial of Service (DDoS) attack. The intentional paralyzing of a computer network by flooding it with data

Detective controls. A form of risk treatment, detective controls identify events while they are taking place

Digital certificate. A digital certificate is an electronic document that uses a digital signature to bind a public key with an identity—information such as the name of a person or an organization, their address, and so forth.

Digital signature. A digital signature is a mathematical scheme for demonstrating the authenticity of a digital message or document.

Directive controls. A form of risk treatment, directive controls provide instructions, and can therefore only be procedural

Disaster Recovery. The activity of recovering telecommunications, ICT, or systems due to a business disruption

Distributed DDoS attack. The intentional paralyzing of a computer network by flooding it with data sent simultaneously from many individual computers

Diversity. The ability to use, select, or switch between different circuits to avoid congestion or network failure

Domain. A domain is a common network grouping, under which a collection of network devices or addresses is organized.

Encryption. Encryption is the process of encoding messages (or information) in such a way that eavesdroppers or hackers cannot read it, but authorized parties can.

Evaluation. The act of making a judgment about the amount, number, or value of something

False negative. An indication that something has been detected or has happened when in fact it has not happened

False positive. An indication that something has not been detected or has happened when in fact it has happened

Fault tolerance. Devices that are designed and built to correctly operate even in the presence of a software error or failed components

Firewall. A firewall is a technological barrier designed to prevent unauthorized or unwanted communications between computer networks or hosts.

Governance. The action or manner of controlling a process

Grey hat. A term generally applied to a hacker who may operate on the boundaries of legality, finding security weaknesses uninvited

Hardening. Hardening is the process of securing a system by reducing its surface of vulnerability.

Message digest or hash function. A hash function is a derivation of data used to authenticate message integrity.

Identification. The process of confirming the identity of an individual or entity

Identity. The fact of being who or what a person or entity is

Impact or consequence. The outcome of an incident that affects assets

Information security. Information security is the practice of defending information from unauthorized access, use, disclosure, disruption, modification, perusal, inspection, recording or destruction.

Integrity. The property of ensuring that information can be altered only by authorized persons, entities, or processes

Interception or eavesdropping. Interception or eavesdropping is the act of secretly listening to the private conversation of others without their consent.

Intrusion. An unwanted or unauthorized access to an information system

Key logger. A key logger tracks (or logs) the keys struck on a keyboard, typically in a covert manner, so that the person using the keyboard is unaware that his or her actions are being monitored.

Legal. Controlled on the basis of statutory law

Likelihood. The possibility that an event may happen

Malware. Any form of software designed to cause harm

Network sniffer. A hardware device or software program capable of logging information on a network

Nonrepudiation. The ability to prove that a person, entity, or process cannot deny having carried out an action

Partitioning. The division of a large network into a number of smaller subnetworks

Penetration testing. Penetration testing is a method of evaluating the computer security of a computer system or network by simulating an attack from malicious outsiders and malicious insiders.

Personal data. Information relating to an individual who can be identified either from that data or from that and other data

Phishing. Phishing is the act of attempting to acquire information such as usernames, passwords, and credit card details (and sometimes, indirectly, money) by masquerading as a trustworthy entity in an electronic communication.

Physical controls. Physical controls consist of anything that places a physical barrier between an attacker and their target.

Policy. A principle or rule to guide decisions and achieve rational outcomes

Preventative controls. A form of risk treatment, preventative controls stop things from happening, and therefore they are implemented before the event.

Privacy. Privacy implies personal control over personal information.

Private key cryptography. A cryptographic system in which identical keys are used both to encrypt and decrypt information

Probability. The extent to which an event is likely to occur, measured by the ratio of the favorable instances to the whole number of possible instances

Procedural controls. Procedural controls consist of standards, guidelines, policies, and procedures.

Procedure. A list of steps which taken together, constitute the instructions for doing or making something

Process. A sequence of events that result in an outcome, and which may consist of a number of procedures

Protocol. A set of rules that define how two entities communicate effectively

Public key cryptography. A cryptographic system in which nonidentical keys are used to encrypt and decrypt information. One key is made public and the other is kept secret.

Qualitative risk assessment. A subjective form of risk assessment that does not use specific values, but that may encompass a range of values

Quantitative risk assessment. An objective form of risk assessment based on numerical values

Redundancy. The inclusion of extra components, which are not strictly necessary to functioning, in case of failure in other components

Regulatory. Controlled on the basis of nonstatutory rules

Resilience. The ability of an organization to counter the effect of business disruptions

Risk. The combination of consequences of a threat occurring and the likelihood of it doing so

Risk acceptance or risk tolerance. A form of risk treatment involving an informed decision to undertake a risk when compared with the organization's risk appetite

Risk appetite. The maximum level of risk that an organization is prepared to accept

Risk assessment. The process of identifying, analyzing, and evaluating risks

Risk avoidance or risk termination. An informed decision not to undertake, or to cease, an activity in order not to be susceptible to a risk

Risk matrix. A mechanism that allows risks to be plotted by impact and likelihood to illustrate the severity and to determine the priorities for risk treatment

Risk modification or risk reduction. A form of risk treatment involving the modification of risk

Risk register. A database that records relevant information about risks and can be used both for reporting purposes to track risk treatment

Risk sharing or risk transfer. A form of risk treatment involving the distribution of risk with other entities, for example insurance

Risk treatment. Once risks have been assessed, they may be treated in one of four ways—acceptance/tolerance, avoidance/termination, reduction/modification, and sharing/transfer.

Rootkit. A rootkit is a stealthy type of software, often malicious, designed to hide the existence of certain processes or programs from normal methods of detection and enable continued privileged access to a computer.

Secrecy. The property that information is prevented from being available or disclosed to unauthorized persons, entities, or processes

Segregation of duties. A procedural control in which one individual undertakes part of an activity and another individual undertakes the remainder

Sensitive personal data. Sensitive personal data include the following: racial or ethnic origin, political opinions, religious beliefs, trade union affiliation, physical or mental health, sexual orientation, and criminal record.

Separacy. A more reliable means of ensuring that specified circuits are not routed over the same cables, equipment, or transmission systems and also that there are no common physical sites within the circuit routings

Social engineering. The act of obtaining confidential information by manipulating or deceiving people

Spyware. Software designed to gather information in a covert manner

Symmetric cryptography. A cryptographic system in which identical keys are used both to encrypt and decrypt information

Technical controls. Technical controls are used to restrict access to sensitive electronic information.

Threat or hazard. A source of potential disruption that has the potential to cause a risk

Trojan horse. A Trojan house is a non-self-replicating type of malware that appears to perform a desirable function but instead facilitates unauthorized access to the user's computer system.

Virtual Private Network. A Virtual Private Network enables a host computer to send and receive data across shared or public networks as if it were a private network with all the functionality, security, and management policies of the private network.

Virus. A virus is a piece of software that can replicate itself and spread from one computer to another.

Vulnerability. The property of something that results in susceptibility to a threat or hazard, and that can result in a business disruption with a consequential detrimental outcome

White hat. A computer security expert or ethical computer hacker, often employed to carry out penetration testing

Worm. A worm is a stand-alone malware computer program that replicates itself in order to spread to other computers.

Zero day exploit. A zero day exploit is an attack that exploits a previously unknown vulnerability in a computer application, meaning that the attack occurs on "day zero" of awareness of the vulnerability.

These definitions vary slightly from the "standards" definitions in order to avoid any conflict of copyright. However, they are closely based on those that can be found in the following international standards:

ISO Guide 73:2009—Risk management—Vocabulary

ISO/IEC 27000:2009—Information technology—Security techniques—Information security management systems—Overview and vocabulary

ISO 22301:2012—Societal security—Business continuity management systems—Guidance

Bibliography

There are many books on cybersecurity-related topics. Here is a sample of those that the reader might find of interest.

Cybersecurity

Alexander, D., A. Finch, D. Sutton, and A. Taylor. 2013. *Information Security Management Principles*, edited by A. Taylor. 2nd ed. Swindon, England: BCS. ISBN 978-1-78017-175-3

Bartlett, J. 2015. *The Dark Net*. London, England: Windmill Books. ISBN 978-0-09959-202-0

BCS: The Chartered Institute for IT. n.d. *Personal Data Guardianship Code*. Swindon, England: BCS. http://www.bcs.org/upload/pdf/pdgc.pdf

Day, P. 2014. *Cyber Attack: The Truth about Digital Crime, Cyber Warfare and Government Snooping*. London, England: Carlton Books. ISBN 978-1-78097-533-7

The European Network and Information Security Agency. 2010. *The New User's Guide: How to Raise Information Security Awareness*. Luxembourg: ENISA. ISBN 978-9-29204-049-9

Goodman, M. 2016. *Future Crimes: Inside the Digital Underground and the Battle for Our Connected World*. London, England: Corgi. ISBN 978-0-55217-080-2

Green, J.S. 2015. *Cyber Security: An Introduction for Non-Technical Managers*. London, England: Routledge. ISBN 978-1-47246-673-0

Hafner, K., and M. Lyon. 1998. *Where Wizards Stay up Late: The Origins of the Internet*. New York, NY: Simon & Schuster. ISBN 978-0-68483-267-8. This book covers the beginnings of the ArpaNet and its eventual transition to the Internet.

IT Governance Institute. 2006. *Information Security Governance: Guidance for Boards of Directors and Executive Management*. 2nd ed. Retrieved from http://www.isaca.org/knowledge-center/research/documents/information-security-govenance-for-board-of-directors-and-executive-management_res_eng_0510.pdf

Lohr, S. 2015. *Data-ism: Inside the Big Data Revolution*. London, England: Oneworld. ISBN 978-1-78074-518-3

Rowlingson, R. 2011. *The Essential Guide to Home Computer Security*. Swindon, England: BCS. ISBN 978-1-90612-469-4

Schneier, B. 2015. *Data and Goliath: The Hidden Battles to Collect Your Data and Control Your World.* New York, NY: W W Norton. ISBN 978-0-39335-217-7

Singer, P.W., and A. Friedman. 2014. *Cybersecurity and Cyberwar: What Everyone Needs to Know.* Oxford, England: Oxford University Press. ISBN 978-0-19991-811-9

Stoll, C. 1991. *The Cuckoo's Egg. Tracking a Spy Through the Maze of Computer Espionage.* London, England: Bodley Head. ISBN 978-1-41650-778-9. This book describes the first major incidence of cyber espionage.

Sutton, D. 2013. "The Issue of Trust and Information Sharing and the Question of Public Private Partnerships." In *Critical Information Infrastructure Protection and Resilience in the ICT Sector,* eds. P. Theron, and S. Bologna (pp. 258–276). Hershey, PA: IGI Global. doi:10.4018/978-1-4666-2964-6.ch013

Sutton, D. 2014. *Information Risk Management.* Swindon, England: BCS. ISBN 978-1-78017-265-1

Sutton, D. 2015. "Trusted Information Sharing for Cyber Security Situational Awareness." *Elektrotechnik und Informationstechnik* 132, no. 2, pp. 113–116. doi: 10.1007/s00502-015-0288-3. ISSN 0932-383X.

Sutton, D. 2017. *Cyber Security: A practitioner's guide.* Swindon, England: BCS. ISBN 978-1-78017-340-5

Business Continuity and Disaster Recovery

Estall, H. 2012. *Business Continuity Management Systems: Implementation and Certification to ISO 22301.* Swindon, England: BCS. ISBN 978-1-78017-146-3

Hastings, R. 2016. *Planning Cloud-Based Disaster Recovery for Digital Assets: The Innovative Librarian's Guide.* Santa Barbara, CA: Libraries Unlimited. ISBN 978-1-44084-238-2

Hiles, A., and P. Barnes. 1999. *The Definitive Handbook of Business Continuity Management.* Chichester, England: John Wiley & Sons. ISBN 978-0471986225

Hotchkiss, S. 2010. *Business Continuity Management: A Practical Guide.* Swindon, England: BCS. ISBN 978-1-90612-472-4

Maiwald, E., and Sieglein, W. 2002. *Security Planning & Disaster Recovery.* New York, NY: McGraw-Hill/Osborne. ISBN 978-0-07222-463-4

Snedaker, S. 2007. *Business Continuity & Disaster Recovery for IT Professionals.* Burlington, NY: Syngress Publishing. ISBM 978-1-59749-172-3

Toigo J. 1996. *Disaster Recovery Planning For Computers and Communication Resources.* Upper Saddle River, NJ: Prentice Hall. ISBN 978-0-13046-282-4

Wallace, M., and L. Webber. 2018. *The Disaster Recovery Handbook.* New York, NY: AMACOM. ISBN 978-0-81443-876-3

About the Author

David Sutton's career spans more than 50 years in information and communications technology. At Telefónica O2 UK he was responsible for ensuring the continuity and restoration of its core cellular networks, and he represented the company in the UK electronic communications industry's national resilience forum.

In December 2005 he gave evidence to the Greater London Authority enquiry into the mobile telecoms impact of the 7/7 London bombings.

He is the author of a number of books on information security and has been a tutor for the Royal Holloway University of London's distance learning MSc in information security.

Index

Acceptable use, 87
Access control, 87, 138, 142
   failures, 48
Account monitoring and control, 135
Accountability controls, 143
Active system, 98
Adjust stage, 6–7
Administrative policies, 87
Administrative privileges, use of, 134
Adobe Acrobat portable document
       format (pdf), 37, 73
"Agile" development, 45
Alerting and invocation processes, 74
Amazon, 29
Antivirus software, 89, 91
Apple, 30
Application software security, 133
Argonite, 94
Ashley Madison, 38
Assets
   information. *See* Information assets
   management, 137
Asynchronous replication, 99
Atlanta's Hartsfield-Jackson
       airport, 94
Audit
   and accountability controls, 143
   functions of, 121–122
   logs, maintenance, monitoring, and
      analysis of, 134
Authentication, 10
   controls, 143
Authorized and unauthorized devices,
      inventory of, 131–132
Authorized and unauthorized
      software, inventory of, 132
Availability, 9–10
Awareness and training controls, 143

Backup and restoral policy, 90
Big data, 36
Biometric methods, 10

Bitcoins, 55
Bluetooth, 92
Bot herders, 54
Botnets, 54
Boundary defense, 134
Briefing cards, 73
Bring Your Own Device, 92
British Airways (BA), 94
British Standards Institute, 4
BS 11200:2014, 160
BS ISO/IEC 27021:2017, 153
BS ISO/IEC 27033-6:2016, 154
Business cases, 21–22
Business continuity
   communication
      dealing with media, 106–108
      information sharing, 104–105
      organization and closely linked
         parties, 105–106
   and cybersecurity, embedding
      general awareness training,
         123–127
      skills training, 127–130
   disaster recovery
      data/information recovery, 95–96
      operating system and application
         recovery, 96–97
      platform disaster recovery, 97–99
   disruptive incidents, response to,
      99–100
      escalation, 102
      incident management process,
         100–101
      management qualities required,
         103–104
      recording events, 102–103
      reporting, 102
   failure timescales, 79–81
   planning and preparation
      continuity requirements analysis,
         84–86
      policies and procedures, 86–93

Business continuity (*continued*)
    plans, 71, 75
    solutions to cyber issues, 93–95
    timeline, 81–83
        immediately following the
            incident, 83–84
        prior to the disruptive incident, 83
Business Continuity Institute (BCI),
        5–6
Business continuity management
        process, 84
    and cybersecurity, 3
    Good Practice Guidelines, 5–6
    guidelines, 5
    information security terminology
        authentication, 10
        availability, 9–10
        confidentiality, 9
        integrity, 9
        nonrepudiation, 10
    meaning of, 1–2
    Plan-Do-Check-Act, 6–7
    reasons for organizations practicing,
        2–3
    recommendations, 5
    senior management buy-in,
        importance of, 3
    specifications, 4
    standards, 4
    terminology
        continuity requirements analysis, 9
        maximum tolerable data loss, 8
        maximum tolerable period of
            disruption, 7
        Minimum Business Continuity
            Objective, 8
        recovery point objective, 8
        recovery time objective, 7–8
Business-critical information, 58
Business impact analysis, 84, 121, 128
Business-impacting cyber incidents, 42
Business resumption plans, 71, 76

Catastrophe, 81
Certification. *See* ISO/IEC 27001
        certification; ISO 22301
        certification
Chain of consequence, 14–15

Change control policy, 89
Classification, 87
Cloud service, 41, 90–91, 92
Cold standby platforms, 97
Commercial in confidence, 87
Communication
    and consultation, 20–21
        business cases, 21–22
    dealing with media, 106–108
    information sharing, 104–105
    organization and closely linked
        parties, 105–106
    security, 139–140
    test
        cost and time vs. complexity,
            113, 114
        description of, 111, 113
        formatting of, 115–116
        frequency of, 113
        participants in, 113
        process to be tested, 112, 113
Communications-Electronics Security
        Group (CESG), 162
Complexity
    communications test, 114
    full exercise, 114
    partial exercise, 114
    simulation, 114
    walk-through test, 113–114
Compliance, 141–142
Compromised system, 92
Confidentiality, 9
Configuration
    data, 38
    management controls, 143
Contact information, 76
Context establishment, 13–14
Contingency planning controls, 144
Continuity requirements analysis, 9,
        84–86
Continuous vulnerability assessment
        and remediation, 132
Control access, 134–135
Cooling systems, 94
Copyright violation, 30
Corporate communications/
        organization's Press
        Office, 115

Corrective controls, 67
Corrective risk treatment, 20
Crises, 80
    management, 100
Critical Security Controls Version 5.0,
        68–69
    account monitoring and control, 135
    administrative privileges, use of, 134
    application software security, 133
    audit logs, maintenance, monitoring,
        and analysis of, 134
    authorized and unauthorized
        devices, inventory of,
        131–132
    authorized and unauthorized
        software, inventory of, 132
    boundary defense, 134
    continuous vulnerability assessment
        and remediation, 132
    control access, 134–135
    data protection, 135
    data recovery capability, 133
    hardware and software, secure
        configurations, 132
    incident response and
        management, 135
    malware defenses, 132
    network devices, secure
        configurations for, 134
    network ports, protocols, and
        services, limitation and
        control of, 134
    penetration tests and "red team"
        exercises, 136
    secure network engineering, 135
    security skills assessment and
        training, 133
    wireless access control, 133
Cryptography, 138
Cyber bullying. See Cyber harassment
Cyber harassment, 31–32
Cyber incidents, 1
    business-impacting, 42
Cyber issues, solutions to, 93–95
Cyber surveillance, 33
Cyber threats, 53–54
    errors and failures, 57
    hacking, 57–58

    loss of key information and IP and
        financial theft, 58
    malware, 54–55
    misuse and abuse, 56–57
    social engineering, 55–56
Cyber vulnerabilities, 47–48
    access control failures, 48
    data stripping, 51
    internet of things, 51–53
    operational management failures,
        49–50
    people-related security failures,
        50–51
    physical and environmental
        failures, 49
    systems acquisition, development,
        and maintenance procedures,
        48–49
Cyber warfare, 32–33
Cyberattacks. See also Cybercrime;
        Cyber threats; Cyber
        vulnerabilities
    external, 17
    internal, 17
Cybercrime, 25
    copyright violation, 30
    dark patterns, 31
    defined, 26
    Denial of Service and Distributed
        Denial of Service attacks, 29
    exploitation, 28
    financial theft, 27–28
    intellectual property theft, 29–30
    website defacement, 28
Cybersecurity, 22–23, 25–26
    and business continuity, 3
        benefits of, 123
        general awareness training,
            123–127
        skills training, 127–130
    Critical Security Controls Version
        5.0. See Critical Security
        Controls Version 5.0
    cyber harassment, 31–32
    cyber surveillance, 33
    cyber warfare, 32–33
    cybercrime
        copyright violation, 30

Cybersecurity (*continued*)
  dark patterns, 31
  defined, 26
  Denial of Service and Distributed
    Denial of Service attacks, 29
  exploitation, 28
  financial theft, 27–28
  intellectual property theft, 29–30
  website defacement, 28
  failures, 33–34
  ISO/IEC 27001 controls. *See* ISO/
    IEC 27001 controls, for
    critical security
  NIST Special Publication 800-53
    Revision 4. *See* NIST, Special
    Publication 800-53 Revision 4

Dark patterns, 31
Data
  entry validation, 49
  journey of, 35–38
  protection, 135
  recovery, 95–96, 133
  stripping, 51
  transfers, 80
Denial of Service (DoS) attack, 29
Detective controls, 65
Detective risk treatment, 19
Direct Attached Storage (DAS), 96
Directive controls, 67
Directive policies for acceptable use, 87
Directive risk treatment, 20
Disaster, 81
Disaster recovery (DR), 11
  of business-critical systems, 49
  data/information recovery, 95–96
  operating system and application
    recovery, 96–97
  platform disaster recovery, 97–99
  recovery plans, 71, 75
Disruptive incidents, response to,
    99–100
  escalation, 102
  incident management process,
    100–101
  management qualities required,
    103–104
  recording events, 102–103
  reporting, 102

Distributed Denial of Service (DDoS)
    attack, 29

EBay, 29
Electronic versions of plans, 72
Environmental failures, 49
Equifax, 26–27
Errors and failure threats, 57
Escalation, 102
Event, 80
Exploitation, 28
External audit, 121
External IT systems, 85
External review, 120
Extrinsic vulnerabilities, 15–16

Facial recognition, 10
Facilitator, 114
Failure timescales, of business
    continuity, 79–81
Federal Information Processing (FIPS)
    standards, 150, 161
FedEx, 55
Financial impact, 42–43
Financial loss projection, 43
Financial statements, 38
Financial theft, 27–28, 58
Fingerprint authentication, 10
Fire detection and prevention
    measures, 94
First-time "offences," warnings for, 44
Force majeure, 100
Forward planning, 115
Full exercise
  cost and time vs. complexity, 113, 114
  description of, 112, 113
  formatting of, 115–116
  frequency of, 113
  participants in, 113
  process to be tested, 112–113

Glitches, 80
Global Domestic Product, 25
Good Practice documents. *See* Good
    Practice Guidelines (GPG)
Good practice guidelines (GPG), 5–6,
    149–150
  Communications-Electronics
    Security Group, 162

Information Security Forum, 162
National Institute of Standards and
    Technology, 161
United States Computer Emergency
    Readiness Team, 162
Guidelines, defined, 5

Hacking, 57–58
Hardware and software, secure
    configurations, 132
High availability systems, 99
Hot standby/high availability
    platforms, 98
Hoy standby systems, 98
Human resource security, 137

Identification and authentication
    controls, 144
Impact Team, 38
Impacts, 14–17
    financial, 42–43
    legal and regulatory, 44
    operational, 44–45
    reputational, 43–44
    on well-being of people, 45–46
Incident, 80
Incident management plans, 70–72,
    74–75
    format of, 72–73
    generic plan contents, 74
Incident management process,
    100–101
Incident manager, appointing,
    103–104
Incident response
    and management, 135
    response controls, 144
Inergen, 94
Information and Communication
    Technology (ICT), 124
    configuration information, 76–77
    experts, 115
Information and intellectual property,
    38–39
Information assets
    cloud services, 41
    information and intellectual
        property, 38–39
    journey of data, 35–38

physical environment, 40–41
processes, 39–40
staff, 39
supply chain, 41
technology, 40
Information hierarchy, 36
Information lifecycle process, 37
Information recovery, 95–96
Information security
    aspects of business continuity
        management, 141
    incident management, 141
    organization of, 136–137
    policies, 136
    terminology
        authentication, 10
        availability, 9–10
        confidentiality, 9
        integrity, 9
        nonrepudiation, 10
Information Security Forum (ISF),
    162
Information sharing, 104–105
Information Technology (IT), 40
Information/cybersecurity staff, 115
Infosec Institute, 51
Insurance claim procedures, 119
Integrity, 9
Intellectual property (IP)
    information and, 38–39
    theft, 29–30, 58
Intelligent personal assistants
    (IPAs), 52
Internal audit, 121
Internal review, 119–120
International Monetary Fund, 25
International Standards
    Organisation, 39
Internet, 81
Internet Engineering Task Force, 150
Internet of Things (IoT), 51–53
Internet Service Providers, 81
Intrinsic vulnerabilities, 15
Invocation process, 101
ISO 22300:2014, 158
ISO 22301:2014, 159
ISO 22301 certification, 120
ISO 22313:2014, 159
ISO 22316:2017, 159

ISO 22318:2015, 159
ISO 22320:2011 Ed 1, 159
ISO 22322:2015, 159
ISO 22324:2015, 160
ISO 22325:2016, 159
ISO/IEC 17788:2014, 157
ISO/IEC 17789:2014, 157
ISO/IEC 24762:2008, 157, 159
ISO/IEC 27000:2017, 150
ISO/IEC 27001 certification, 120
ISO/IEC 27001 controls
    access control, 138
    asset management, 137
    communications security, 139–140
    compliance, 141–142
    cryptography, 138
    human resource security, 137
    information security aspects
        of business continuity
        management, 141
    information security incident
        management, 141
    information security policies, 136
    operations security, 139
    organization of information
        security, 136–137
    physical and environmental security,
        138–139
    supplier relationships, 140
    system acquisition, development,
        and maintenance, 140
ISO/IEC 27001:2017, 150
ISO/IEC 27001/27002 controls,
    69–70
ISO/IEC 27002:2017, 150
ISO/IEC 27003:2017, 150
ISO/IEC 27004:2016, 151
ISO/IEC 27005:2011, 151
ISO/IEC 27006:2015, 151
ISO/IEC 27007:2017, 151
ISO/IEC 27008:2011, 151
ISO/IEC 27009:2016, 151
ISO/IEC 27010:2015, 151
ISO/IEC 27011:2016, 152
ISO/IEC 27013:2015, 152
ISO/IEC 27014:2013, 152
ISO/IEC 27015:2012, 152
ISO/IEC 27016:2014, 152

ISO/IEC 27017:2015, 152
ISO/IEC 27018:2014, 153
ISO/IEC 27019:2017, 153
ISO/IEC 27031:2011, 153, 159
ISO/IEC 27032:2012, 153
ISO/IEC 27033–1:2015, 153
ISO/IEC 27033–2:2012, 154
ISO/IEC 27033–3:2010, 154
ISO/IEC 27033–4:2014, 154
ISO/IEC 27033–5:2013, 154
ISO/IEC 27034-5:2017, 155
ISO/IEC 27034-6:2016, 155
ISO/IEC 27034–1:2011, 154
ISO/IEC 27034–2:2015, 154
ISO/IEC 27035-1:2016, 155
ISO/IEC 27035-2:2016, 155
ISO/IEC 27035:2011, 155
ISO/IEC 27036–1:2014, 155
ISO/IEC 27036–2:2014, 155
ISO/IEC 27036–3:2013, 155
ISO/IEC 27037:2016, 156
ISO/IEC 27038:2016, 156
ISO/IEC 27039:2015, 156
ISO/IEC 27040:2016, 156
ISO/IEC 27041:2016, 156
ISO/IEC 27042:2016, 157
ISO/IEC 27043:2016, 157
ISO/IEC 27050-3:2017, 157
ISO/IEC 29100:2011, 158
ISO/IEC 29101:2013, 158
ISO/IEC 29190:2015, 158
ISO/IEC 30111:2013, 158
ISO/IEC29147:2014, 158

K.I.S. principle, 103

Led Zeppelin, 30
Legal and regulatory impact, 44
"Light-touch" audit, 117
Likelihood, 16, 17–18
Lockheed-Martin, 30, 33
Loss of key information, 58

Maintenance
    controls, 144
    of plans, 118–119
Malware, 54–55, 89
    defenses, 132

protection up-to-date, failure to
    keep, 50
Maximum tolerable data loss
    (MTDL), 8, 81
Maximum tolerable period of
    disruption (MTPD), 7, 83
Media, 100
    dealing with, 106–108
    protection controls, 145
Meltdown and Spectre, 34
Minimum business continuity
    objective (MBCO), 8, 83
Misuse and abuse threats, 56–57
MTPoD. *See* Maximum tolerable
    period of disruption (MTPD)

National Institute of Standards and
    Technology (NIST), 88
    Draft Cyber Security guides, 160–161
    good practice guidelines, 161
    SP 800-53 Revision 4, 70, 71
        access control, 142
        audit and accountability, 143
        awareness and training, 143
        configuration management, 143
        contingency planning, 144
        identification and
            authentication, 144
        incident response, 144
        maintenance, 144
        media protection, 145
        personnel security, 145
        physical and environmental
            protection, 145
        planning, 145
        program management, 147
        risk assessment, 146
        security assessment and
            authorization, 143
        system and communications
            protection, 146–147
        system and information
            integrity, 147
        system and services
            acquisition, 146
    National Technical Authority for
        Information Assurance, 162
    Network Attached Storage (NAS), 96

Network devices, secure
    configurations for, 134
Network ports, protocols, and
    services, limitation and
    control of, 134
Networks, of organization, 94–95
Nonrepudiation, 10
NotPetya, 55

Observers, 115
Operating system and application
    recovery, 96–97
Operational controls, for risk, 67–68.
    See also specific controls
Operational impact, 44–45
Operational management failures,
    49–50
Operations security, 139
Organization-approved training
    courses, 129

Paper-based documentation, 72
Partial exercise
    cost and time vs. complexity,
        113, 114
    description of, 112, 113
    formatting of, 115–116
    frequency of, 113
    participants in, 113
    process to be tested, 112, 113
PAS 77:2006, 160
Passcode, for authentication, 10
Passwords
    for authentication, 10
    length of, 88
    policies, 89
    recommendations on, 88
"Patch gap", 91
Patent infringement, 30
PD 25111:2010, 160
PD 25666:2010, 160
PD ISO/TS 22317:2015, 159
Penetration tests and "red team"
    exercises, 136
People-related security failures, 50–51
Personal information, 38
Personnel security controls, 145
Petya struck, 55

Phishing attacks, 56
Physical and environmental
    protection controls, 145
Physical and environmental security,
    138–139
Physical controls, 67–68
Physical environment, as information
    asset, 40–41
Physical measures, 20
Physical security, 94
    defects, 49
Plan-Do-Check-Act, 6–7
Planning and preparation
    continuity requirements analysis,
        84–86
    policies and procedures, 86–93
Planning controls, 145
Plans
    incident management. *See* Incident
        management plans
    maintenance of, 118–119
    review of, 119–121
    testing and exercising
        benefits to organization of,
            109–110
        conditions for, 110
        format for, 115–118
        people involved in, 113, 114–115
        reasons for, 109
        requirements for, 109
        types of, 111–113
Platform disaster recovery, 97–99
Policies and procedures, 86–93
Power, 93
Preventative controls, 65
Preventative risk treatment, 20
Prevention, 61. *See also* Strategic
    options; Tactical, and
    operational solutions
    cost of, 3
    fire detection and, 94
Probability, 16
Procedural controls, 67
Procedural measures, 20
Processes, as information asset,
    39–40
Program management controls, 147

"Quick wins", 86

Ransomware, 54–55
Recommendations, defined, 5
Recording Events, 102–103
Recovery point objective (RPO), 8,
    81
Recovery time objective (RTO), 7–8,
    81
Redundant Array of Inexpensive
    Disks (RAID), 96
Regulatory impact, 44
Remote access, 91
Removable media, 89–90
Reporting, 102
Reputational impact, 43–44
Requests For Comment, and
    the International
    Telecommunications Union
    standards, 150
"Residual" risk, 19
Review of plans, 119–121
Risk
    accept/tolerating, 19, 64
    analysis, 17
    appetite, 14
    assessment, 14–19, 146
    avoid/terminating, 18–19
    environment, general view of,
        12–13
    evaluation, 18
    identification, 14
    management process
        business cases, 21–22
        communication and consultation,
            20–21
        context establishment, 13–14
        defined, 11
        monitoring and review, 22–23
        used in, 11
    matrix, 17–18
    meaning of, 12–13
    reduce/modifying, 19, 64
    share/transferring, 19, 62, 64
    treatment, 19–20, 64
Robust network monitoring, failure to
    ensure, 50
Rootkits, 54

Scraping technique, 51
Secure network engineering, 135

Security assessment and authorization controls, 143
Security awareness training
    benefits of, 123–125
    methods to deliver, 125–126
    outcome of, 126–127
Security requirements, 41
Security skills assessment and training, 133
Segregation of duties, 90
Senior management buy-in, importance of, 3
Shaky web interface, 52
Shared network drives, 90
Simulation exercise
    cost and time vs. complexity, 113, 114
    description of, 111–112, 113
    formatting of, 115–116
    frequency of, 113
    participants in, 113
    process to be tested, 112, 113
Singapore Standards Council, 4
Skills training, 127–130
    methods of, 129–130
    requirement of, 127–128
Social engineering, 55–56
Software, updating, 48–49, 91
Solid State Drives (SSDs), 92
Spam, 56
Specifications, defined, 4
Spirit, 30
Spoofing attacks, 56
Spyware, 54
Staff, as information asset, 39
Standard "office" software applications, 73
Standards, 149
    business continuity, 158–161
    defined, 4
    ISO/IEC 27000 series standards, 150–157
    relevant ISO standards, 157–158
"Standby" system, 98
Storage Area Networks (SANs), 91, 96
"Storyboard" technique, 125
Strategic options, 62–65
Strategic risk management process, 63

Subject matter experts, 115
Supplier relationships, 140
Supply chain, as information asset, 41
Symmetric warfare, 32
Synchronous replication, 99
System acquisition, development, and maintenance, 140
System and communications protection controls, 146–147
System and information integrity controls, 147
System and services acquisition controls, 146
Systems acquisition, development, and maintenance procedures, 48–49

Tactical, and operational solutions
    operational controls, 67–68
    tactical controls, 65–67
Tactical controls, for risk, 65–67. See also specific controls
Team members, roles and responsibilities of, 74
Technical controls, 68
Technical measures, 20
Technology, as information asset, 40
Termination of access permissions, 89
Testing and exercising plans, 109
    benefits to organization of, 109–110
    conditions for, 110
    format for, 115–118
    people involved in, 113, 114–115
    reasons for, 109
    requirements for, 109
    test and exercise, distinction between, 110
    types of, 111–113
"The full story", 107
Third-party relations, 45
Threats, 14
    assessments, 59
    cyber. See Cyber threats
Timeline, business continuity, 81–83
    immediately following incident, 83–84
    prior to disruptive incident, 83
Transmission Control Protocol (TCP), 80

Uber, 28
Uninterruptible power source
    (UPS), 93–94
United Nations, 25
United States Computer Emergency
    Readiness Team (US-CERT),
    162
User Datagram Protocol (UDP), 80
User password management, 48
Users' access rights, 48

Violation of copyright, 30
Viruses, 89
Vulnerabilities, 15–16
    assessments, 59
    cyber. *See* Cyber vulnerabilities

Walk-through test
    cost and time vs. complexity,
        113–114

description of, 111, 113
formatting of, 115–116
frequency of, 113
participants in, 113
process to be tested,
    112, 113
WannaCry virus, 55
Warfare, 32
Warm standby systems, 98
Web-based survey tool, 125
Website defacement, 28
Well-being of people, impacts on,
    45–46
Wireless access control, 133
Wireless networking and mobile
    devices, 91–92
World Bank, 25

"Zero-day" vulnerabilities, 91

OTHER TITLES IN OUR INFORMATION SYSTEMS COLLECTION

Daniel J. Power, University of Northern Iowa and DSSResources.com, *Editor*

- *Creating a Culture for Information Systems Success* by Zakariya Belkhamza
- *Information Technology Security Fundamentals* by Glen Sagers and Bryan Hosack
- *Building Successful Information Systems: Five Best Practices to Ensure Organizational Effectiveness and Profitability, Second Edition* by Michael J. Savoie
- *Computer Support for Successful Project Management: Using MS Project 2016 with Construction Projects* by Ulhas M. Samant
- *Decision Support, Analytics, and Business Intelligence, Third Edition* by Daniel J. Power and Ciara Heavin
- *Successful ERP Systems: A Guide for Businesses and Executives* by Jack G Nestell and David L Olson
- *Computer Support for Successful Project Management: Using MS Project 2016 with Information Technology Projects* by Ulhas Samant

Announcing the Business Expert Press Digital Library

Concise e-books business students need for classroom and research

This book can also be purchased in an e-book collection by your library as

- *a one-time purchase,*
- *that is owned forever,*
- *allows for simultaneous readers,*
- *has no restrictions on printing, and*
- *can be downloaded as PDFs from within the library community.*

Our digital library collections are a great solution to beat the rising cost of textbooks. E-books can be loaded into their course management systems or onto student's e-book readers. The **Business Expert Press** digital libraries are very affordable, with no obligation to buy in future years. For more information, please visit **www.businessexpertpress.com/librarians**. To set up a trial in the United States, please email **sales@businessexpertpress.com**.